Living with Bereavement

For all the people whose
stories and insights I have
woven into this book –
with grateful thanks.

LION

Living with Bereavement

Sue Mayfield

ISBN 978 0 7459 5295 6

First edition 2008
10 9 8 7 6 5 4 3 2 1 0

Typeset in 10/12 Classical Garamond
Printed and bound in China

Text acknowledgments

Special thanks are due to all the people who
agreed to tell their stories and share their
experiences – many of whose names have been
changed for the sake of privacy. I am deeply
grateful to them for their honesty and wisdom.
Thanks to Ken Edwards and Ann Barnardo
from Cruse Gloucestershire and to Sue Major
at Winston's Wish for their professional
expertise and helpful feedback; to Sheilagh
Banner and Venetia Hopkins for reading the
text; and to Jerry Gilpin for kindly allowing the
publication of his poem 'Scattering'.

pp. 46, 60–61, 94, 123 Extracts from *New
Journeys Now Begin* © 2006 Tom Gordon,
published by Wild Goose Publications.

p. 53 Extract from 'We say the dead depart' by
David Constantine from *Collected Poems*
(Bloodaxe Books, 2004).

pp. 94–95 'I am with you always' by Sue Wallace
from *Wise Traveller – Loss*, published by Scripture
Union, 2007. Permission granted by the author.

p. 106 Extract from 'Empty Wardrobes' by Douglas
Dunn from *Elegies* published by Faber & Faber, 1985.

pp. 115–16 'Time Does Not Bring Relief' copyright
© 1917, 1945 by Edna St. Vincent Millay.
Reprinted by permission of Elizabeth Barnett,
Literary Executor, the Millay Society.

Scripture acknowledgments

pp. 16, 21, 33, 38, 46, 66, 71, 77, 83, 88, 96, 99,
105 Scripture quotations are from the New Revised
Standard Version published by HarperCollins
Publishers, copyright © 1989 by the Division of
Christian Education of the National Council of the
Churches of Christ in the USA, and are used by
permission. All rights reserved.

p. 89 Scripture quotation taken from the Holy
Bible, New International Version, copyright ©
1973, 1978, 1984 International Bible Society.
Used by permission of Zondervan and Hodder &
Stoughton Limited. All rights reserved. The 'NIV'
and 'New International Version' trademarks are
registered in the United States Patent and
Trademark Office by International Bible Society.
Use of either trademark requires the permission of
International Bible Society. UK trademark number
1448790.

pp. 93, 117 Scripture quotations are from the
Contemporary English Version published by The
Bible Societies/HarperCollins Publishers, copyright
© 1991, 1992, 1995 American Bible Society.

Contents

When Someone Dies

Only the unloved and unloving escape grief.
CLAIRE RAYNER, FOREWORD TO *THROUGH GRIEF*

All of us, at some time in our lives, experience the death of someone we love. The way we respond will be different for each of us. Bereavement is a universal, inescapable reality but it is also a uniquely personal voyage.

What happens when you die?

The way we respond when someone dies depends on how we think of death. This will be shaped by our life experience, our philosophical framework and our religious beliefs. To some people, death is an absolute end, the extinguishing of life. For others it is a continuation of life in a different dimension, the start of a spiritual 'afterlife', even a homecoming. Alfred Tennyson, in his poem 'Crossing the Bar', pictures death as a boat carrying us over a sandbar into a world we cannot see – a comforting metaphor, or a piece of Victorian sentimentality, depending on your point of view.

Some think of death as a natural process, part of our life cycle – something simultaneously ordinary and mysterious, like birth. Others think of death as *un*-natural – the interloper in the garden, an aberration, a corruption of the original created order, something to 'rage, rage' against, as Dylan Thomas says in his poem 'Do Not Go Gentle Into That Good Night'.

'We are rightly offended by death,' says Tom Gordon, reflecting on his work as a hospice chaplain. The seventeenth-century poet John Donne shares this sense of offence, seeing death as an enemy that will ultimately be defeated and overcome:

One short sleepe past, wee wake eternally,
And death shall be no more; death, thou shalt die.
'DEATH BE NOT PROUD'

Whatever our point of view, many of us are confused and uncertain about death. So much is unknown and unknowable. What exactly happens? If souls live on after death, then where are they? Can they

see us? We might hedge our bets a bit, like eighteenth-century poet Robert Burns:

> *If there's another world,*
> * he lives in bliss;*
> *If there is none,*
> * he made the best of this.*
>
> 'EPITAPH ON A FRIEND'

But however we understand death, and whatever we believe about afterlife or non-afterlife, the sense of loss is inescapable. Bereavement is messy and painful, and there is no way round that. The person we love is not there any more and we are bereft. Even if we have faith that the person is in a better, more fulfilled, less anguished place, we still feel their absence like an aching void.

Who, what and how?

Although the experience of bereavement is common to all, the dimensions and 'shape' of our grief and the particular emotions it gives rise to will vary depending on who has died and how. What age were they? What were the circumstances of their death? How were we connected to them? Was their death what we would consider a 'good death' (if such a thing exists)?

The death of a parent, grandparent, spouse, child, sibling or friend will all feel different. If we have been especially close to the person who has died, we are likely to experience more intense grief. If we have been estranged or distant, our sadness may be complicated by feelings of guilt, regret or remorse. If a baby dies, or a father of young children commits suicide, or an elderly person is murdered, we may be overwhelmed by a sense of unfairness, rage or despair. When a woman dies at eighty-five after a long and fulfilled life, we may feel less sense of turmoil and outrage than when an eighteen-year-old boy is killed in a road accident. But old age won't necessarily make death more bearable. Bill – a man who had faced the death of his mother and father early in life and described himself as largely 'unaffected' by them – found himself (in his mid-fifties) completely unseated by the death of his 89-year-old stepfather, a man he had grown to love and admire over many years.

Bereavement can be a chaotic cocktail of emotions. When we are bereaved we experience huge mood swings and heightened sensitivities. Our normal protective 'skin' feels thinner. In families, this chaos may be amplified by the clashing of several personalities working through their bereavement in different ways with conflicting emotional needs. A death can sometimes cause feelings connected to earlier losses and sorrows to resurface and complicate the picture yet further. The period following a death is a time of extremes when we may feel as if we're on a rollercoaster.

'Getting through a bereavement is like riding a bucking bronco,' says journalist Virginia Ironside, '... it's all we can do to keep our fingers gripped to its mane. And just hope we don't fall off.'

What are the rules?
In writing about bereavement, and in talking to all the people who have contributed to this book, I have become acutely aware of two things: that all bereavements are different, and that with grief (as with so many other things) there is no such thing as 'normal'.

> *One person wants to be private, another to shout from the rooftops; one finds physical comfort and loads of hugs and kisses a comfort, others shrink away, hiding like a wounded animal.*
> VIRGINIA IRONSIDE

The way I grieve will not be the same as the way you grieve, but there is no right or wrong way to do it. There are no rules when it comes to loss – no blueprint for what is appropriate or expected. As writer Mary Stott says, 'In grief we do as we must.'

But this very lack of a template can leave us feeling bewildered and lost. Largely speaking, the outward customs and etiquette of mourning that used to shape our behaviour and demeanour – drawn curtains, doffed caps, lowered flags or the wearing of black armbands – have all but disappeared. We no longer tear our clothing or put ashes on our heads as the Old Testament prophets did or withdraw from public life wearing 'widow's weeds' as Queen Victoria did. The shapeless emotional muddle that we are left with can seem overwhelming – especially when those around us sometimes seem chiefly concerned with our 'getting over it'.

Stages and patterns?

Bereavement experts have identified stages, or phases, that a person may go through after a death, as a way of unravelling this muddle and making sense of the chaos. In 1972 psychiatrist Colin Murray Parkes described a four-stage progression of numbness-pining-disorganization-recovery. A few years earlier, psychiatrist and author Elisabeth Kübler-Ross had outlined five stages of death and dying: denial-anger-bargaining-depression-acceptance. Some bereavement counsellors work with a three-stage model of shock-adjustment-reinvestment in life. This idea of 'grief stages' can be unhelpful if applied too literally or too rigidly. It may cause me anxiety that I am not progressing through the stages in the 'right order' or resentment at the implication that I am seen as behaving predictably or 'typically'. But it can also be useful – if only in giving me a sense that I am not going mad! Elisabeth Kübler-Ross defined her 'stages' as ways of marking out grief's terrain – tools to help us frame and identify what we may be feeling – and as such they are valuable. They can act as waymarkers, delineating an alien landscape.

What use is a book?

I hope that this book will help in mapping out some of the emotions you are likely to encounter in bereavement.

I realize that in some ways, books are useless. Several people told me that for months – even years – after being bereaved they couldn't actually concentrate to read a book. Others said that books – particularly the sort filled with glib platitudes – filled them with rage. Trying to write a book that will help and not annoy is a tall order given that we are all so different. Some people may be genuinely comforted by the frequently quoted words of the Oxford theologian Henry Scott Holland that 'Death is nothing at all' and 'All is well.' But others may want to yell 'Rubbish! Death is *every*thing – it is complete devastation!'

And anyway, as Virginia Ironside wisely observes:

> *When you're bereaved you're so all over the place that you might find a book heart-warming on a Tuesday and mindless nonsense on a Wednesday.*

Many people, however, said that reading other people's stories was useful and gave a sense of perspective and hope. Patrick, whose wife Joanna died of cancer, found that reading about other people whose life partners had also died of cancer helped him to grasp that 'everybody dies' and that 'death is utterly irreversible'. Sheilagh, talking about the deaths of her father, her mother and her fourteen-year-old son, said, 'Books where I could find echoes of myself were helpful.'

I hope, then, that this book, and the glimpses of other people's lives that it gives, will be valuable as a touchstone for those weathering a bereavement. I hope too that it will help to make sense of bereavement's terrain for the non-bereaved – those on the edge looking in and feeling helpless to be of comfort and support. No one can ever really say that they know how someone else is feeling. We just don't. But the more we understand the dynamics of bereavement, the better we will be at accompanying each other.

And finally...

Alongside anecdotal material and insights about the dynamics of grief and loss I have included quotations from the Bible and short reflections from within the Christian tradition. I recognize that

many people reading this book will not share my own Christian perspective. The quotations from the Old and New Testaments are included not to suggest that Christians have all the answers about death, but rather because they seem powerfully to express the pain of human grief and our longing for comfort and meaning. They also speak of a God who suffers with humanity and who has, in the person of Jesus, himself experienced the anguish of death and the transforming miracle of resurrection. There is undoubtedly a tension within Christianity – which I will revisit in the chapter on 'Faith and Hope' – between death and resurrection, the permanent and the impermanent, heaven and earth, which many Christians grapple to hold in balance. Jim, a Catholic priest, writing in his journal after taking the funeral of a teenage boy with cerebral palsy, expresses this very honestly.

> *For the Christian death is always a bitter contradiction – utter devastation at loss but the deep knowledge that what we see as death is a mere shadow cast on the reverse side of true life.*

If the Bible quotations provide some comfort or strike chords with your own feelings, good. If they rub you up the wrong way, just skip them. If the book annoys you on a Tuesday, come back to it on a Wednesday. And if you are too distracted or sad to read at all, just look at the pictures.

Shock and Anticipation

Why should a dog, a horse, a rat have life,
And thou no breath at all?
WILLIAM SHAKESPEARE, *KING LEAR*, ACT V, SCENE 3

Death is usually a shock, whatever the circumstances – even if the person who dies is very old. Gordon, who cared for his 97-year-old friend Maurice, said this:

> *Given his age I had prepared myself for the likelihood of Maurice's death, but it was still a shock to go out to the shops and to come back home and find him dead.*

Even when death is expected there may still be an element of shock. Hope nursed her mother Edwina for the last few weeks of her life as she died of a brain tumour and was shocked by the rapid changes she saw. 'It was like sand rushing through my fingers – I was unable to stop it,' she said. Edwina, an active 88-year-old and a prolific writer, felt as though she had been cut off mid-sentence – that her approaching death was too soon and too sudden.

If a person's death has been sudden or traumatic the sense of shock may be even greater. Jonathan's brother Simon died when the car he was driving left the road and hit a tree. Because Simon's death was so unexpected Jonathan's sense of shock was profound.

When death breaks into the ordinary 'out of the blue', it is particularly hard to deal with. Louise, who is in her thirties, was getting ready for a night out – rushing to bath her two small children before the arrival of the babysitter – when her husband Andrew suddenly developed a severe headache. He died a short time later from a massive brain haemorrhage.

ෆ৪৩

Death from suicide brings a very particular sense of shock. The UK charity Winston's Wish recognizes this and runs special camps for children bereaved as a result of suicide. On the BBC Radio 4 programme *Woman's Hour*, Di Stubbs from Winston's Wish described the aftermath of suicide as 'grief with the volume turned up'. Rosemary, now in her eighties, recalls her father's suicide, when she was just fourteen:

> *He shot himself with his World War I revolver. I remember saying to my parents, when I was playing in the attic the day before, 'The gun's gone.' It was an awful shock. I had no chance to say goodbye.*

The impression bereaved people have of the world being upside down – of 'time being out of joint', as Hamlet says – seems all the greater when someone dies young. Losing a child can feel as if the natural sequence of life has been disrupted. In the Old Testament, King David, hearing of the death of his son, grieves terribly:

> *The king covered his face and... cried with a loud voice,*
> *'O my son Absalom, O Absalom, my son, my son!'*
> 2 SAMUEL 19:4

Joan's daughter Marion died after suffering from multiple sclerosis for many years. Marion was forty-two; Joan is in her seventies. 'It's the wrong way round,' Joan said, describing ordering her daughter's headstone.

Dave and Jackie knew, when their son Nigel joined the Parachute Regiment, that there was a chance of him being killed.

16

When he was eighteen he narrowly escaped death in Northern Ireland, but three years later he died in the Falklands War. 'As soon as I heard,' Dave said, 'I experienced an almost physical click in my brain. I went into autopilot – like my emotions were frozen.'

Many people I interviewed described the physical and psychological effects of this first wave of shock. Dave's wife Jackie said, 'I closed off. It was like going into a bubble. I felt like I had cotton wool in my ears.' Several people talked of blankness. Penny, whose twelve-year-old daughter Molly died in a road accident, said, 'I shut down. I was very efficient. I dealt with the police and calmly told the friends who'd come to supper what had happened.' Hyper-efficiency and the ability to keep functioning without emotion in the first hours and days after a bereavement is common and is part of the body's normal reaction to shock.

The body has a safety mechanism [numbness] that protects us from the tidal wave of emotion that might otherwise push our heart rate and blood pressure up to a physically dangerous level.
DR TONY LAKE

Several people described a surreal sense of timelessness. Nick – whose wife Esther died of cancer at 39, leaving him with four young children – talked about amnesia and a sense of 'time loss'. Four years on, he struggles to remember much about the first year after Esther's death.

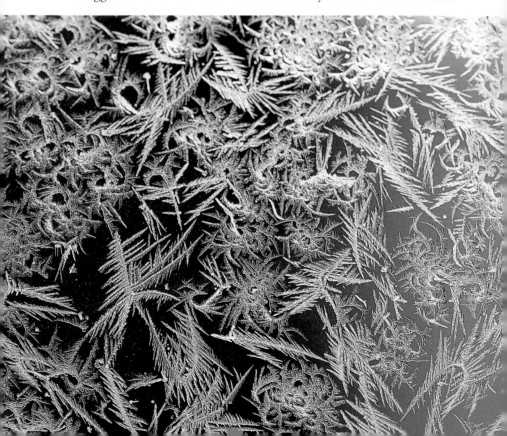

Val experienced shock as a feeling of euphoria. Her husband – a fit man in his late sixties – died of a heart attack after singing the song 'Goodbye' (from the musical *White Horse Inn*) during a New Year's dinner. Val describes her feelings at the time as strangely serene, almost joyful, and remembers being energetic and talkative in the first days and weeks after his death. Her euphoria was heightened by the sense that his had been a 'good death'. 'He died within minutes with no suffering and he'd had a lovely evening doing the things he loved,' she said. 'The title of the song he was singing seemed particularly appropriate...'

Like Val, Patrick considered the death of his wife Joanna to have been a 'good death'. Diagnosed with terminal cancer in her late sixties, she and Patrick had several months to prepare themselves and to grieve together at the loss of their anticipated future. They were able to talk openly about her death, and Patrick feels Joanna reached the point where she was 'ready to die'.

Nick's wife Esther also had time to prepare herself and others for her death. She wrote letters to their four children and to Nick and spent precious time with family and friends. She also made many practical arrangements that helped keep the household afloat after she died. Nick was grateful for the detailed information doctors gave about the likely course her illness would take and felt that this reduced his sense of shock.

When an illness is long or predictable the process of grieving often begins in anticipation. Grieving *before* someone's death doesn't necessarily lessen the pain or shock when death finally comes, but it may familiarize a person with some of the feelings they will experience. Jane talked of grieving for her father for several years before his death as his health deteriorated and his life became curtailed. A man whose wife had Alzheimer's disease described losing her 'piece by piece'.

But what if the anticipation just creates a sense of protracted suffering? Actress Sheila Hancock, in her poignant book about the death of her husband John Thaw, writes about the agony of witnessing his declining health:

He is fading. I want to pull him back. Force him to stay. I want to scream don't leave me…

And what if the desire to prepare for death and say goodbye isn't shared by the dying person? What if they can't or won't face the truth of what is happening?

Ros's husband Greg had oesophageal cancer, and though their nurse told Ros it was terminal, Greg refused to discuss his death. 'He was a great fighter,' Ros said. 'He wanted to beat it. I wanted him to write letters to the children but he couldn't do it.'

Joan's daughter Marion, a multiple sclerosis sufferer who spent the last four years of her life in bed, had so much suffering and so little quality of life that eventually Joan prayed for her to die. 'It was terrible. I was asking for something that I didn't want to happen but sometimes you know death is better for a person really,' she said. When Marion finally died Joan was glad that the last word she had said to her was 'goodnight'.

Goodbyes can make a big difference to the people left behind. Grace died of a heart condition at eleven days old. When it was clear that she wouldn't live, the hospital staff encouraged her parents to unhook her from the drips and monitors and take her out on the seafront in her pram so that they had some memories of being together as a family. A very compassionate photographer – who had himself lost a baby – took photographs of Grace and her parents. These, and the memory of this day of leave-taking, gave them some comfort after she died.

• •

Jesus anticipated his crucifixion in the Garden of Gethsemane. He experienced great fear at what lay ahead and a sense of isolation as his friends – unable to fully comprehend what he was going through – fell asleep.

> … *he withdrew from them about a stone's throw, knelt down, and prayed. 'Father if you are willing, remove this cup from me; yet, not my will but yours be done.' Then an angel from heaven appeared to him and gave him strength. In his anguish he prayed more earnestly, and his sweat became like great drops of blood falling down on the ground. When he got up from prayer he came to the disciples and found them sleeping because of grief…*
> LUKE 22:41–45

Funerals and Ceremonies

The day you bury him is a day of chores and crowds, of hands false or true to be shaken, of the immediate cares of mourning. The dead friend will not really die until tomorrow, when silence is round you again.

ANTOINE DE SAINT-EXUPÉRY

For a lot of bereaved people a funeral is something to be 'got through' – a hurdle they have to jump before the real grieving can begin. Many people spoke of functioning on 'autopilot' up to and during the funeral. Everything felt unreal: they had a sense of standing outside themselves watching things happening; looking back it was all a blur. For Sarah, whose father died two days before her wedding, there was a harsh sense of irony. The family had to change gear to organize a funeral when she should have been getting ready for her wedding.

For many families, planning and discussing a funeral service gives a positive focus. It can be a bonding experience and may even be tinged with hilarity. Sarah recalls getting the giggles in the lift at the registry office at the absurdity of cancelling her wedding on one floor and registering her father's death on another! 'Gallows humour' is often a necessary safety valve and part of the shock reaction that follows a crisis event.

Patrick described the process of devising his wife Joanna's funeral as absorbing and creative. He was glad to be busy and to have a clear task. For others, this time of decision-making and activity is too rushed and frenzied.

22

∞੪৪০

A funeral is a complicated event. What exactly is it? Is it a celebration of the life of the person who has died or a chance to express grief that they are gone? Is it a 'send off' or a collective opportunity to lament? Is it chiefly for the dead person or for those left behind? Should the focus be on the sorrow of this life or the hope of the life to come?

Most of us will have been to bad funerals and good ones. Bad ones are often hurried, impersonal, 'one size fits all', with little involvement from the dead person's family or friends and no space for private thoughts. Bad funerals really do feel like something to be endured. Good ones, by contrast, are more personal, tailored to the character of the person, accommodating of the mixed emotions people bring to the service, and rich in laughter and tears.

Val talked enthusiastically about her husband's funeral:

Charles always loved a good funeral! [At his] The music was wonderful. It brought the family together and I was in awe at the number of people who came. It was a January day but at one point it seemed as though the whole church lit up and glowed – like a glimpse of God's glory.

Getting the balance right between grieving and celebrating is never easy. I have been to Christian funerals which leaned so far towards rejoicing in the promise of heaven that there was no space to be sad, angry or bewildered. I have also been to funerals that felt more like episodes of *This is Your Life* than acknowledgments of the reality of death. Some people get around this tension by having two occasions, a funeral and then a memorial service – the first to focus on grief, shock and loss; the second to celebrate the person's life.

Nick opted for a two-part ceremony when his wife Esther died. The low-key funeral, just a few days after her death, was raw and harrowing; the memorial service three months later was a much larger event – more reflective, more carefully crafted and more joyful. Having planned the second service with a group of friends and family, Nick experienced a rush of pleasure when it all 'came together', which was deeply cathartic.

Patrick found the fact that his wife had left no instructions whatsoever for her funeral very helpful. It gave him freedom to do what seemed most appropriate without worrying about whether it was exactly what she would have wanted.

For others, fulfilling someone's plans can give a sense of purpose to the first few days and weeks of bereavement. Esther Rantzen, in her foreword to the book *How to Have a Good Death*, says this:

My late husband knew his heart disease was likely to shorten his life, and left me a running order for his memorial service, which enabled me to carry out his wishes, and was the last gift of love I was able to give him.

24

In Western culture, and especially in Britain, funerals are often quite undemonstrative affairs, the emotions in evidence modest or well concealed. For some of us this is our upbringing – we believe that public displays of *any* emotion are unseemly. For some, it is the effects of shock that can give mourners a glazed, disconnected look or make them unusually 'hyper' or socially adept. But for many people, 'holding it together' at the funeral is a conscious strategy, an act of the will. This might be out of concern for others.

Val said, 'My grandchildren were there and my daughter was distraught. I had to be strong for her.' Sarah, at her father's funeral, wanted to be 'strong' for her mother; she felt that was what her dad would have wanted. But she was also terrified of going to pieces. 'I had a fear that if I lost it, it would be overwhelming,' she said.

Other cultures do things differently. Gordon described attending a Kenyan funeral where there was loud wailing and everyone threw earth onto the coffin as it was lowered into the ground. As a British man in his seventies, he found this uninhibited demonstration of sorrow quite unsettling. Hope, on the other hand, found that attending an emotional burial in a Turkish village some months after her own mother's funeral gave her an opportunity to weep in ways in which she hadn't previously been able.

There is great cultural variety in the way we view and deal with a person's body after their death, too. At the Kenyan funeral Gordon described, the dead man's body was viewed, touched, kissed and wept over by his family and friends for several hours before the lid was put on the coffin. In the West, we are often less comfortable with a person's corpse. Indeed, many of our funeral practices deliberately conceal or beautify the body – perhaps to shield us from the reality of death.

Some people choose not to see a body after death. They may prefer to remember the person living rather than dead, or they may feel the body no longer *is* the person. One woman said of her friend's body, 'It was just a tattered overcoat that she no longer needed.'

For some people, however, contact with the body is necessary. Sheilagh talked about how important it was for her to stay with her fourteen-year-old son Tom after his death. 'I sat with his body – holding him – until the undertaker came a few hours later,' she said. Between his death and the funeral Sheilagh and her ten-year-old

daughter visited the chapel of rest everyday to be with Tom. Tom's sister wrote a message to put in the coffin along with a selection of toys that she had chosen for him.

For Penny, whose twelve-year-old daughter Molly died in a car accident, having Molly's embalmed body in the house for the days leading up to the funeral was helpful. During this time Molly was dressed in her favourite clothes and friends put daisy chains in her hair. Penny found sitting beside her daughter's body with friends and neighbours very consoling.

The involvement of children in the funeral preparations of both Tom and Molly is in stark contrast to the

stories of many elderly people. Gordon's father died when he was nine and he wasn't allowed to go to the funeral despite wanting to. 'I was sent to a neighbour's house and watched the funeral go by from the front window,' he said. Experts emphasize the importance of allowing children to make their own choices: *Do I want to see Grandma's body or not? How do I want to say goodbye to Daddy?*

Not seeing someone's body or not being able to have, or attend, a funeral can cause problems for bereaved people of any age. In a war or in major disasters such as 9/11 or the 2004 tsunami, in which retrieval of bodies is impossible, the absence of human remains often makes grieving more complicated.

Jackie found it difficult that, when her son Nigel died in the Falklands, his body was buried on the islands. Six months later, however – in response to public demand – the bodies of Nigel and his colleagues were disinterred and brought back to the UK for a second burial. Jackie said:

> *When his coffin came back I wanted to take the lid off but I couldn't – obviously. Never having seen his body was the hardest thing. For quite a long time afterwards I thought that maybe they'd made a mistake and he'd just got lost somewhere. If I'd seen his body I'd have **known**.*

Linda had a miscarriage several years ago and lost a baby boy whom she named John. Because of the circumstances she didn't see his body and was unable to have a funeral. 'I had a sense of things being unfinished,' she says now.

When someone is buried there is a concrete place to visit:

> *The advantage of a cemetery is that there is no expectation for people to stay composed, nor to appear as if they have "got over" the death... Cemeteries can therefore provide much-needed relief from the everyday mask that many people may be wearing for some time after the death of a loved one.*
>
> JANE FEINMANN

Sheilagh finds her son Tom's grave both comforting and agonizing:

> *At first I visited weekly, then monthly and now I go a few times a year. I don't really think he's **there** but his bones are there and that's the nearest thing to physical contact. We always go early on Christmas morning and take him a Christmas tree. Still – even now, twelve years later – I find it hard to walk away from his grave.*

Joan, whose daughter Marion died two years ago, visits Marion's grave about once a fortnight. She has planted flowers there and likes to garden quietly when she visits. But her other daughter, Claire, chooses *not* to go to her sister's grave. 'She says Marion isn't really there, and that she prefers to think of her somewhere else,' Joan says.

But what if the person who has died is cremated? What happens to his or her ashes? As with so many things, there is no blueprint. Some bereaved people choose to scatter or inter ashes in a special place soon after the funeral. Others hang on to them for much longer.

Carol carried out her husband's wishes to have his ashes scattered in the Scottish Highlands. She travelled with her mother-in-law a few months after his death and they scattered them together, but, wanting to be more private, Carol kept some ashes back and went again a year later to complete the process alone.

After the death of my friend's father, her mother divided his ashes into several paper parcels and their large family went together to a favourite wood at daffodil time. This poem was written about the occasion:

Scattering

*Beneath the bright cold ridges of cloud
the ashes drifted softly away,
and on the fleshy leaves of daffodils
grit pattered and bounced.*

*The rain held off. Coats buttoned,
we played hide and seek through the ruins
till the children's faces shone red
and their breath smoked in the chill air.*

The kind of day you shared and relished:
conversation you struggled to break into;
photographs that refused to be composed –
the sprawling life of your family.

Briefly, we stopped our laughter, stood in line
to say our thank-yous, formal and shy
like children after a party,
clutching their small bags of sweets and toys.

There was enough of you for all of us:
A grey and silver handful each
for your children and grandchildren,
gathered along a paling fence in the damp woods.
JERRY GILPIN

Louise feels much more ambivalent about her husband's ashes. A year after his death they are still in storage at the crematorium. 'They're not really *him* and yet they *are* him,' she says. 'I miss his physical presence and they are the last trace of it. I want to scatter them somewhere open and free but I'm not sure where. I wanted to do it before the first year was up but I also don't want to rush it...'

Nick feels a similar sense of 'unfinished business' about his wife Esther's ashes, which he still has, four years after her death. He says, 'I haven't wanted to deal with them – partly because I couldn't decide what to do or where, but partly because of not wanting to let them go. Once they are gone they are gone...'

Penny waited eight years before she felt ready to bury the ashes of her daughter Molly. When she finally did, it gave her a sense of peace. 'It was symbolic of a new phase of grieving,' she said. 'It's allowed us to move on.'

Waiting for the right moment was important for several people

I spoke to. One woman regretted that her father's ashes had been hastily interred on the day of his funeral in a soulless crematorium plot. Twenty-five years on she wanted to do something with her brothers to give a physical focus to their feelings about the traumatic changes that had followed their father's death. She suggested they each write about how they had felt, burn the paper to create 'ashes', then put *these* in the ground under a newly planted tree.

Sometimes – when circumstances have been less than ideal or where there is no body to bury – resourceful alternatives to funerals can give some sense of completion and peace. Tom Gordon, a hospice

chaplain, recalls a gay man called Steve who – unacknowledged by his partner Grant's family and therefore excluded from Grant's funeral – had no opportunity to mourn publicly or conventionally. Steve devised his own ritual. Taking a treasured object (a gift from Grant) and a letter he had written to his dead partner he went to the Scottish borders. He describes the experience in the book *New Journeys Now Begin*:

> *High up in the hills, he went slightly off the path and in a quiet spot with a glorious view he buried the gift and the letter, made a little cairn of stones, and sat and wept.*
>
> TOM GORDON

• •

King David, hearing news of the death of his enemy Saul and his dear friend (Saul's son) Jonathan, marked his grief with public acts of mourning:

> *Then David took hold of his clothes and tore them; and all the men who were with him did the same. They mourned and wept, and fasted until evening for Saul and for his son Jonathan...*
>
> *David intoned this lamentation over Saul and his son Jonathan...*
>
> *'Your glory, O Israel, lies slain upon your high places...*
> *How the mighty have fallen in the midst of the battle!*
> *Jonathan lies slain upon your high places.*
> *I am distressed for you, my brother Jonathan; greatly beloved were you to me; your love to me was wonderful, passing the love of women.'*
>
> 2 SAMUEL 1:11, 17, 19, 25–26

Disbelief and Disorganization

I found myself within a dark wood
Where the straight way was lost...
DANTE ALIGHIERI, *THE DIVINE COMEDY: INFERNO*

Part of the shock of bereavement can be a sense of disbelief. 'This can't really be happening. It doesn't seem real. Any minute now I'll wake up and it will all have been a bad dream...'

Disbelief is often intensified if a death is sudden or unexpected or the person is very young. John and Diana's daughter Debbie died of an asthma attack at the age of twenty-four. She had visited them the evening she died. 'Debbie and her husband Paul were going out for an Indian meal,' John said. 'When Paul phoned a few hours later to say she'd died, the news didn't sink in.'

Louise, whose husband died quickly and suddenly from a brain haemorrhage, said this:

> *Andrew was always so ALIVE! He believed that life is for living and was bursting with energy. Even when he was dead he was glowing with health. I find it hard to believe, even now...*

Several people I spoke to who had lost partners talked about their expectation that their husband or wife would come home. This was especially acute for those whose partners often travelled with their work. 'I kept thinking he was just away on a trip and would come back,' said one widow. 'Even now I feel as if he's just away for a while. It would be so lovely to see him walk back through the door.'

Joan wrote a poem after her daughter Marion's death that expresses her own sense of dismay and disbelief:

*For me, the world is standing
   still,
And everything seems so
   unreal;
I feel that I'm just standing
   by
Unseen, unheard, and
   wondering why.*

It is common for bereaved people
to be disorganized and
dysfunctional. They can't seem to
get things done – can't process
information, can't concentrate.
Even simple tasks seem beyond
them.

Hope, dealing professionally
with a traumatic terrorist incident
in a foreign city only a few
months after her mother's death,
found herself unable to find her
hotel room at the end of the day.
'I went back to the hotel and got
into the lift but I couldn't find my
way to the right level. I was
exhausted,' she said.

Claire was forgetful after her
sister died and had difficulty
making simple decisions. At times
she struggled to string a sentence
together.

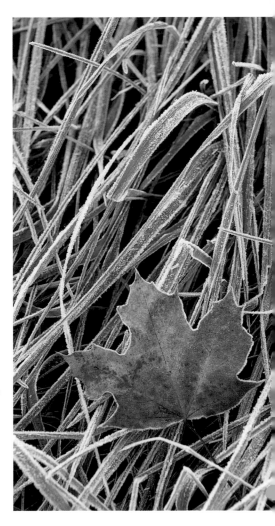

❦

For family and friends who have nursed an ill person for months, or even years, the loss of routine after that person dies can bring a sense of disarray. Patterns of domestic care – the comings and goings of nurses and doctors – are disrupted by death, and the shapeless emptiness of a household afterwards can leave a bereaved carer feeling disorientated and lost. In addition, the riot of emotions that accompany bereavement can bring an alarming sense of disorder. For some this will feel as though everything is exaggerated: you have a loss of perspective so little things loom larger than usual; you lose your temper or get upset more easily; you need greater reassurance or take offence more quickly; you appear to have misplaced your sense of humour.

For others, chaos and disorder bring a sense of flatness and pointlessness. C. S. Lewis, writing about his feelings after the death of his wife, registers a vague sense of wrongness, of something amiss. 'What's wrong with the world,' he writes, 'to make it so flat, shabby, worn-out looking?' He also experiences grief as a muffled, dislocated, cut-off sensation:

> *No one ever told me that grief felt so like fear... The same fluttering in the stomach, the same restlessness... At other times it feels like being mildly drunk, or concussed. There is a sort of invisible blanket between the world and me.*

Sheilagh experienced a feeling of blankness after her son Tom died. A practising Catholic, she went to Confession some months after Tom's death and told the priest she was worried that she didn't feel anything. He was reassuring and told her to plant some seeds and watch them grow.

Disbelief and disorganization may last weeks, months, or even years. However long they last they are perfectly normal.

Elisabeth Kübler-Ross, in her book *On Grief and Grieving*, writes about feelings of depression and pointlessness and an intense fog of sadness which are, she says, '... a way for nature to keep us protected by shutting down the nervous system so that we can adapt to something we feel we cannot handle'.

• • • • • • • • • • • • • • • • • • • •

The book of Ecclesiastes in the Old Testament recognizes that there will be times in our lives that are destructive as well as constructive, when things fall apart and crumble around us.

> *For everything there is a season, and a time for*
> *every matter under heaven:*
> *... a time to mourn, and a time to dance;*
> *a time to throw away stones, and a time to gather*
> *stones together...*
> *a time to keep, and a time to throw away;*
> *a time to tear, and a time to sew...*
> ECCLESIASTES 3:1, 4, 5, 6, 7

Absence and Presence

Be with me always – take any form – drive me mad!
Only do not leave me in this abyss where I cannot find you!
HEATHCLIFF IN *WUTHERING HEIGHTS*

Whatever we believe about heaven, or God, or the souls of the dead, when someone dies we experience their *absence*. They were there, and now they are not. Their presence – at least their physical, human, bodily presence – has gone, and our relationship with them is interrupted. As Jonathan said about his brother Simon after his sudden death, 'He's just *not there*!' Our dismay at this absence is perhaps linked with our bafflement about death. We wonder how someone can be there one minute and gone an instant later.

Absence can feel intolerable – like a wailing ache, a black hole, an empty shell, a vacuum. Sheilagh, whose son Tom died aged fourteen, said this: 'It was like having nothing in your middle – just this huge emptiness… I used to long for Tom and ache with the lack of him.'

Actress Sheila Hancock writes harrowingly about the hours after her husband's cremation:

When they'd gone, I howled like an animal, prowling round, looking for traces of him. I can still smell him but he has absolutely gone. Utter despair at his absence, his total absence. I feel as though a whole part of me has been hacked away, leaving a bleeding gaping wound.

Psychologists identify this sense of utter desolation as 'separation anxiety', a normal part of our psychological make-up – a fear of abandonment developed in infancy. For a time, a person's absence may completely colour our view of the world. In Shakespeare's play

Antony and Cleopatra, Cleopatra berates Antony for dying and leaving her alone:

> *Noblest of men, woo't die?*
> *Hast thou no care of me? Shall I abide*
> *In this dull world, which in thy absence is*
> *No better than a sty?*
> ACT IV, SCENE 15

Without Antony her world feels ugly and pointless.

CR&O

When someone dies, we miss their physical presence – their touch, their smell, their smile, their voice. We may also miss the way they think or their sense of humour. We might hear or see something funny and long to share it with them. We miss the relationship we had with them: wanting to ask a question that only she would know the answer to; wanting to make a reference that only he would 'get'. Jane, a single woman in her early forties, lived near her elderly parents and kept a close eye on their well-being, having a meal with them once a week for many years. When they died in close succession Jane found she was constantly thinking of things she wanted to tell them. She even found herself unthinkingly driving to their house.

Paradoxically, although there is a sense of absence, there may also be a sense of presence. Patrick's wife Joanna died on their forty-forth wedding anniversary. Remembering her, he says:

> *She was my wife, my lover, my best friend for all those years – so*
> *of course the relationship continues. I talk to her photograph and*
> *it feels natural to do this. I don't expect an answer, of course...*

Talking to someone who has died is natural and common, particularly when the person who has died is your lifelong partner.

Nick described how conversations with his wife Esther continued after she died, especially in the first days and weeks:

> *I chatted to her regularly – especially about the children – and at the start, I had a sense that she reciprocated. It's less frequent now and more internalized – I ask myself, 'What would she feel about this? What would she do? What would she say?'*

Many people talk about a continued sense of a person's presence after death. Rather like the sensations amputees report of still

being able to 'feel' the lost limb, they have a feeling that the dead person is still 'there'. In some cases this is hallucinatory; they seem to *see* the person who has died. Some describe vivid dreams of the person (a subject I'll come back to in the chapter on 'Energy and Sleep'). Some have a sense of a person's voice or words, like Val, who woke one morning with a feeling that her dead husband Charles was bringing her a cup of tea. Hearing a sound, she called out to him and heard him saying, 'I can't stay, I have to go...'

Some people just have a feeling, a sensation, of closeness. Hannah, whose father died just before her fourth birthday, remembers feeling her dad's presence, especially at night. Now seventeen, she says, 'I think he's with me – in my life. I used to

have this sense more strongly. When I was in bed I'd think about him looking down at me and it was comforting.'

Several people said the feeling of 'presence' was most acute at times of decision or difficulty, as if their dead friend or relative was looking out for them or helping them in some way.

We may be sceptical of 'sightings' or feel uncomfortable with the idea of a person speaking from beyond the grave. It may not sit easily with our theology of death. But seeing, hearing and feeling a person after they have died is extremely common and a normal part of grief.

For some, the sense of continuation is more like an ongoing influence. Asking, 'What would Dad think of this?'; thinking, 'Molly would love this'; being aware of someone's taste, their likes and dislikes, their political views, their strengths and weaknesses – all these things give the sense of an unbroken relationship. Sarah, whose father – a keen cricketer – died before her own children were born, describes watching her eighteen-year-old son Jamie play cricket:

I can see the resemblance. Jamie looks like Dad – which is nice. His stance, his body shape, the way he holds his bat is all like Dad. When I watch him I often think, 'Dad would have loved to watch him play.'

Val's husband Charles died twelve years ago, and although she has made many changes since his death the force of his personality continues. 'I still live with a consciousness of his likes and dislikes,' she says. 'I've just built a new summer house and I'd love him to see it.'

For Patrick, the ongoing influence of his wife Joanna is a very poignant thing. 'I get upset by things that Joanna loved or would have loved,' he says.

Continuing presence is part of the agony of absence. The tension between continuity and discontinuity, absence and presence, can be heartbreaking. C. S. Lewis described himself as homesick and hungry after his wife's death:

> *You tell me 'she goes on'. But my heart and body are crying out, come back, come back.*

• •

Christians believe in the 'Communion of Saints' – the unseen
spiritual company of those who have already died. The apostle
Paul writes:

> ... we are surrounded by so great a cloud of witnesses...
> HEBREWS 12:1

Hospice Chaplain Tom Gordon says that this concept of the
Communion of Saints helps us grasp:

> ...both sides of the bereavement coin – the pain of the loss, and the
> continued connectedness with the departed.

Continuity and Routine

If you're going through Hell, keep going.
ATTRIBUTED TO WINSTON CHURCHILL

When someone dies, bereaved people are often immensely resourceful and good at finding coping strategies that keep them afloat. For many, keeping going and keeping busy are lifelines. Maintaining some sense of normality and continuing with everyday rhythms gives a sense of order amongst the chaos.

For Jackie and Dave, whose son Nigel died in the Falklands, going back to work was essential. Work provided safety, company and routine; for them, it was like scaffolding poles holding up a crumbling building.

For many bereaved people, being busy is a welcome break from grief. Linda found, after having a miscarriage, that being occupied with her other children helped her manage and contain the sadness she felt. Penny's husband Mark threw himself into his work after their daughter Molly was killed, as a way of 'anaesthetizing' himself.

Occupation – especially occupation that can be done without too much thought or emotional involvement – can be an oasis. Following the death of his wife Esther, Nick found that getting back to work was vital for his sanity, though his workplace performance was a mixed bag. When it came to 'mindless' paper tasks he found that he was actually *more* efficient than usual. But the aspects of his job requiring 'people skills' were harder, and he reflects – four years on – that he probably made some bad decisions in the wake of Esther's death. Jonathan went back to work as a university researcher a month after his brother's death because he needed the safety net it gave him, although he found poor concentration made work difficult. For a lot of people, returning to paid work very soon after a death is an economic necessity. Whatever the circumstances, balancing practicalities with emotional well-being will be a very individual thing.

∽∗∾

Everybody copes differently. Some bereaved people don't just continue former patterns, they take on additional routines and activities as a way of managing their sense of loss. Carol, who along with her husband Len had been a long-time coach of junior sport, extended her coaching role after Len's death, finding that having responsibility for the young people helped her in her bereavement. 'I felt I had two choices,' says Carol. 'I could sit and mope or get on with life. I know what Len would want me to do – get on and be useful to others!'

But what if picking up the threads of 'normal life' after a bereavement seems impossible, or undesirable, or even appalling? What if the very idea of life going on as before is offensive to you?

For Penny, in the first weeks after the death of her daughter Molly, normality seemed an outrage. 'I found that nothing seemed to matter. My life had stopped – so *everything* should stop! I found eating and drinking difficult and watching others eat and drink disgusted me. How dare they carry on? Life seemed so casual – with people taking everything for granted.'

Louise, whose husband Andrew died of a brain haemorrhage, was ambivalent about the routines that the lives of their two children required. She said:

> *Having small children is a double-edged sword. You have to get on with it – to get up in the morning and function, which keeps you from sinking into oblivion. And yet functioning – even*

*being alive – makes me feel disloyal to Andrew – like one
Siamese twin living on without the other. I almost feel angry at
the children for keeping me here. I don't **want** to be here – I
want to be with Andrew!*

It is easy to become *too* busy after a bereavement. Sarah described
her mother who, unexpectedly widowed at fifty-five, embarked on
a programme of evening classes, new hobbies and clubs:

*She got really tired. The big thing was that she didn't want to
be in the house at six o'clock – the time she used to hear the
click of the gate as Dad came home from work. Gradually –
after getting completely exhausted – she weaned herself off the
clubs and bit by bit got used to being alone in the house.*

Busyness may be desirable but it can also be counterproductive. Virginia Ironside likens constant activity to pressing the 'pause button' on a video – a diversion that simply slows down the process of grieving:

When you stop doing whatever you were doing – going to parties, helping others, seeing movies – you still return to a film which hasn't moved on since you stopped watching it. You can wish and wish you could fast-forward to the end, but you can't.

Driving yourself too hard after a bereavement may be unwise. Penny went back to her job as a district nurse a month after Molly died. 'I never really got on top of my job again though,' she said. 'A year later I completely collapsed and had to be on Prozac for a year.'

Hope accompanied her husband to a new Foreign Office posting very soon after her mother's death and found the pressure of re-locating, briefings and new situations difficult to cope with. 'I felt I'd fall apart if I started to rush around. I couldn't face taking on anything else,' she said.

You may have an urgent need to get back to normal or you may choose to delay and take time out. You might want to keep busy or you might opt to make space to be still. You may choose to cushion yourself from the reality of loss or you may choose to stare loss straight in the face. The way you behave will depend on who you are and how you approach life. 'Stuff to do' can be a distraction that delays grief or it can be a much needed respite break. Only you will know what you need and how to look after yourself.

However we respond it is undeniable that our emotions need a rest from time to time. Bereaved people – and especially bereaved children and teenagers – don't and can't feel sad all the time. In and amongst expressing their feelings they need – perhaps more than ever – all the 'normal stuff' of life such as football,

television, dog-walking, shopping or time with friends.

After a bereavement life *does* carry on. Our feelings will be many and various – sometimes contradictory. Although we might not feel like it much of the time, we may still laugh, we may enjoy food or sex, we may still notice the little things that give us joy. If we keep going 'because it's what he would have wanted', that very continuity is part of our expression of grief.

• •

George Herbert's poem is often quoted:

Laugh and be glad
for all that life is giving,
and I, though dead,
will share your joy in living.
'THOUGH I AM DEAD'

This poem by David Constantine may be less familiar:

And how alive
The world continues to be with things the dead man loved
Last week, goldfinches, say...
'WE SAY THE DEAD DEPART'

Whether we notice them or not, the goldfinches will still be there. And whether we go with the rhythm or rail against its futility, life will go on.

Anger and Guilt

I experienced the most intense anger, bitterness and pain which raced through every part of me, and I shouted a host of expletives. My anger was directed not just at the evil creatures who had planted the bomb but at the injustice of Tim losing such a promising young life.

COLIN PARRY WRITING IN *TIM: AN ORDINARY BOY* ABOUT HIS TWELVE-YEAR-OLD SON TIM, KILLED BY AN IRA BOMB

Sadness is expected when someone dies. Anger may be unexpected, though it is a common and thoroughly normal reaction to bereavement. Some people *may* experience the death of somebody they love with no sense of anger at all, but many will be filled with rage and fury.

If you are feeling angry, your rage may be directed at specific people or things. You may feel angry with the surgeon who failed to keep your friend or relative alive; the driver of the car who caused your daughter's death; the unfairness and waste of an unfinished life; the unanswered questions; the sudden death that left you with no chance to say goodbye.

You may want to blame someone. Dave felt furious with Prime Minister Margaret Thatcher when his son Nigel died in the Falklands War. 'When the war was over I wanted to shout, "What about our sons?" I felt he'd died in a cause that wasn't worth fighting for,' he said.

Christine felt angry with the doctors who treated her husband Pete. 'They didn't seem to know what they were doing and I felt as though they were pulling the wool over my eyes,' she said.

You may even feel angry with the person who has died. Abandoned. Betrayed. Ros, bereaved in her thirties, described feeling angry with her husband Greg for not being there. Dave felt angry with his son Nigel for 'getting himself killed' in the Falklands War.

Anger is often irrational and will sometimes be unfocused and generalized. One woman described her husband, after the death of their daughter, as permanently short-tempered and irritable. You may find yourself on a short fuse – hitting out uncharacteristically. It is common for clergy, undertakers, florists and caterers to feel the lash of misplaced anger during preparations for funerals. Anger within families – often triggered by tactless remarks or casual oversights – may flare. Couples may rail against each other after a child has died, locked in mutual blame or growing distant from each other because of incompatible ways of handling the loss. The high separation rate for couples in the first few years after a child's death is evidence of how difficult grieving together can be. Similarly, sibling rivalries and jealousies may burst out when an elderly parent dies. A mother grieving her dead son may clash with a daughter-in-law grieving her dead husband. They may even – consciously or unconsciously – compete with each other to grieve the more extravagantly.

If you have a religious faith you may feel angry at God. Linda, who had a miscarriage, says she shouted at God in her prayers for many months afterwards. 'Why did God allow it to happen when I had prayed, "Look after this child"?' she said. 'I felt so let down. I had so many questions...' You may even find your faith disintegrating.

If the person you loved has met their own death with rage – like the figure in Dylan Thomas's poem who rages 'against the dying of the light' – you may be left carrying traces of that anger too.

Death can be an angry business. Virginia Ironside reflects on the practice of military salutes at funerals:

At funeral rituals, the American Indians used to shoot spears and arrows into the sky, and at military funerals guns are still fired, in an apparent expression of fury.

The UK charity Winston's Wish gives children and their parents the opportunity to express anger during their bereavement support camps. One woman described the 'Anger Wall':

Children were encouraged to write or draw something that had made them angry and pin it onto the wall. Then they hurled lumps of wet clay at it. Some people got really furious and screamed and yelled as they did it. It was very therapeutic.

Carl and Ruth, who are now stepbrother and sister, were both angry when bereaved as young children. Carl, whose mother died of cancer, bottled up a lot of anger and his schoolwork suffered. Ruth, who was eight when her dad died, was furious when her mother married Carl's father. Ruth's mother described her daughter's reaction:

Ruth was very close to her dad and when he died she missed him terribly. When I met Paul her anger got worse. She'd lost her dad already and now she was losing her mum to another man.

Children often respond angrily to death, and their inability to articulate their fury can make things worse. For some children, bereaved early in life, a sense of suppressed anger will erupt in their teenage years. For those bereaved as teenagers, feelings may be amplified by hormonal changes and normal teenage moodiness.

In the book *How to Have a Good Death*, Jessica recalls how, as a teenager, the seriousness of her father's illness was hidden from her:

When I was thirteen my father died... As I was closer to my dad than to my mum, I reacted by directing all my anger at my mother, openly wishing she was the one who had died instead. Now I am reconciled with my mother but I am angry instead at my father for denying me the opportunity to round off my relationship with him, and for what he must have put my mother through.

Whatever our age, anger is easier to deal with if we can express it without judgment or censure from those around us. This may be easier said than done. Anger is spiky and uncomfortable, and our friends may find our tears easier to deal with than our bile. But having the opportunity to express anger can do us good.

... we live in a society that fears anger. People often tell us our anger is misplaced, inappropriate, or disproportionate. Some people may feel your anger is harsh or too much. It is their problem if they don't know how to deal with it... scream if you need to. Find a solitary place and let it out.

ELISABETH KÜBLER-ROSS

When someone dies as a result of suicide there can be anger of a particularly raw kind. Friends, relatives and carers may feel the dead person has broken ranks and deserted them. They might be furious at what seems like a selfish act. I once attended the funeral of a woman in her thirties from a large and close-knit family. There was such a sense of betrayal at her suicide that the family needed to include in the service a moment when they formally forgave their sister for killing herself. People bereaved by suicide can feel a toxic mix of rage, guilt and self-blame. They feel they should have done more, or that their efforts to support their friend or relative have been rejected. They wish they could have controlled forces they actually had no control over.

CB80

Other deaths bring guilt as well. Jonathan found himself feeling guilty while making a snowman with his toddler son soon after his own 38-year-old brother Simon died. 'I felt bad that Simon's son would never get to make a snowman with *his* dad,' he said. Joan felt guilty for moments of happiness after her daughter died. 'I felt as though I shouldn't being enjoying myself because Marion was dead,' she said. Sarah, whose dad died when she was in her twenties, felt guilty when, six months after his death, she found she couldn't remember exactly what he looked like.

If your relationship with the dead person was fractured or unsatisfactory you may feel guilty for not having tried harder or not having made the effort to be reconciled. A son may feel guilty that he didn't visit his mother before her death. A sister may feel guilty that her brother bore the brunt of their father's illness. Undertakers comment that the most lavish and expensive funerals are often motivated by guilt!

Guilt and self-blame are common reactions to miscarriage or stillbirth. A bereaved mother may feel that her baby has died because she failed to nurture and protect it. She may feel that she shouldn't have gardened, or smoked that one cigarette, or jogged, or eaten a particular type of cheese, or made love to her partner.

Feeling shame is common amongst mothers who have lost

older children too – shame at not having cared for them properly or having failed to protect them from harm.

Sometimes anger, guilt, shame and self-blame can get all tangled up in a messy knot, and a bereaved person needs help unravelling these feelings. One woman described a boy who, when asked to articulate his anger, drew a picture of a bicycle, despite the fact that his big sister had died in a car accident. When questioned by a bereavement support worker his logic emerged: his parents had bought a bike for his sister just before she died and he, feeling jealous, had said mean things to her. After she died, his parents gave the bike to him but he hated it and felt guilty riding it. The bicycle had become a focus for a complicated mix of emotions, and the grieving boy had started to think that his spiteful comments about the bike had somehow caused his sister's death.

• •

People who believe in God can find it useful to express their anger in prayer.

I Rage

I rage at God,
And in my angry shouts I hate his will.
I scream at God,
And in my wails I will disturb his rest.
I rant at God,
And in my raving prayers would have him hear.
I rail at God,
And in my tears and cries I doubt his way.
I curse at God,
And in my lost control offend his ear.

I am with God
What I must be, for now, for this.
I am with God,
Ev'n now, with rage, ev'n now, with God,
I am with God.
Please God, I pray you understand.
TOM GORDON

Regret and Relief

The bitterest tears shed over graves are for words left unsaid and deeds left undone.

HARRIET BEECHER STOWE

When someone dies we may experience regret. Perhaps we regret words we said or didn't say. Perhaps we regret things we did or didn't do. Perhaps we just wish that things had been different – in life as well as in death.

Anne's husband worked overseas. When he died abroad she was left with a sense of regret that his last period of leave had been spoilt by marital arguments. Jonathan and his brother Simon – both married and in their thirties – had drifted apart and rarely saw each other. When Simon died suddenly, Jonathan regretted that they hadn't spent more time together and that the catch-up they were always planning had never happened.

As well as regret for ourselves we may also feel regret on behalf of the person who has died: she didn't live to see her daughter married; he missed his grandson's birth by a week; she never got to make that trip she was planning...

People often regret not being there when someone they love dies. If the circumstances of a death are traumatic or painful, feelings of regret may be all the more intense. Although Lorna's elderly father dearly wanted to die at home, he actually died in a care home, having gone there for a short respite break. His medical condition and the medication he was receiving made him hostile and aggressive. Lorna's last hours with him, as he died, left her feeling that he was angry with her for disobeying his wishes. If last moments, last hours or last conversations have been other than we would have wished, we can be left with feelings that are ragged and unfinished.

The words 'if only' can drive us mad after someone has died: if only she'd caught a later train; if only I'd picked them up from the party myself; if only we hadn't been interrupted by visitors that day he started to say something important...

Writer Blake Morrison, in his book *And When Did You Last See Your Father?*, describes the night after his father's death:

*My mother and I sit by the fire with plates on our knees. We drink wine with the roast chicken, and she begins a litany of **if onlys**: if only my father had had himself checked out regularly;*

if only he'd not refused the barium meal they'd offered him a month ago; if only she'd not had her accident...

Regret, though natural, can be self-destructive. It can gnaw at us and make us bitter and raw. 'Many of us crucify ourselves between two thieves – regret for the past and fear for the future,' said the American writer Fulton Oursler.

Just as worrying can't alter the future so regret can't alter the past. For this reason, some bereaved people make a deliberate choice not to permit themselves to say 'if only...'

Sheilagh's fourteen-year-old son Tom, who had cerebral palsy, died of a fit while in respite care. As Tom had often fitted before,

and Sheilagh was used to dealing with his fits at home, she could easily have blamed the care home for his death:

We did wonder if it would have happened if he'd been at home that day but we quickly stopped this questioning and opted not to go down that road. Everybody was very upset at the care home and I felt I needed to go there to reassure them that it wasn't their fault and that I didn't blame them.

Penny felt the same after her daughter Molly died in a car accident. The car Molly died in was being driven by another woman, who was bringing Molly back from a music lesson. 'I told the driver straight away that I forgave her,' Penny said. 'I knew that if I didn't do it then I never would.'

Deciding to shut the door on regret and 'if-only's may be easier said than done. It might seem unattainably virtuous (since our instinct may well be to lash out bitterly), but forgiveness can also be a form of self-protection. It can cut us free from destructive cycles of recrimination and blame.

In contrast to the torment of regret, many people have feelings of relief when someone dies. This may be relief that a long illness has finally ended, that the person we love is no longer suffering, that there is an end to pain. Or, if a long and happy life has ended with sudden death, there may be relief and gratitude that the person had no suffering or no deterioration of quality of life. Relief and thankfulness for a life well-lived and for a good and peaceful death won't take away the sense of loss bereavement brings, but they may soften it a little.

There can be an enormous sense of relief when death brings an end to a difficult relationship. A man with a domineering mother who was impossible to please may well feel relief when death cuts him free from the tyranny of perfectionism. A woman with a controlling or overbearing husband may find herself coming out from under his shadow when he dies. She may experience not just relief but a new feeling of liberation. Relief of this kind may bring fresh guilt in its wake.

As bereavement is a time of mixed emotions, it is possible that when someone dies we will experience regret *and* relief, and that we may feel guilty for our ambivalent feelings. Whatever our emotions, being honest about them is an important part of grieving and healing.

• •

Because regret and remorse can be corrosive, trying to draw a line under the things that have happened that we cannot change can sometimes be helpful.

In this verse from the Old Testament, the prophet Isaiah speaks words that he believes are God's words:

> Do not remember the former things,
>   or consider the things of old.
> I am about to do a new thing;
>   now it springs forth, do you not perceive it?
> I will make a way in the wilderness
>   and rivers in the desert...
> ISAIAH 43:18–19

Loss and Despair

The pain now is part of the happiness then. That's the deal.
C. S. LEWIS

The more we have loved a person, the more we suffer when that person dies. The closer the connection has been, the more devastating will be the loss. One man, whose wife died after fifteen years of happy marriage, talked of a sense of 'utter, aching loss'.

A widow described the first year after the death of her husband:

I felt as if I was holding on to a slippery rock while the waves lashed against me – feeling like letting go, but gripping on by my fingers' ends.

A mother, reflecting on the death of her daughter, said, 'I felt completely stripped of everything. Nothing seemed to matter.'

Loss will feel different for each of us. Poet and artist Laurence Whistler, in his book *The Initials in the Heart*, describes his feelings after his wife's death as a series of bewildering weather conditions:

> *Thus I entered the hemisphere of loss, which has not a weather of its own but a whole new climate of weathers flowing forward without end. They came over me by day and night, in flying fogs and lights of anguish, gratitude, unbearable or assuaging recollection.*

In addition to the colossal sense of loss of the person we have loved, we may also be mourning the loss of an unrealized future – of lost opportunities or unfulfilled dreams. Hannah, whose father died when she was only three, has an ongoing sense of loss. Now that she is on the brink of adulthood she is aware that he isn't there to witness academic achievements or life events such as first boyfriends, school plays and decisions about career or university. He won't be at her wedding and he won't be there when she has children of her own. She has not only lost her father, she has also lost the grandfather of her children and the potential of an adult friend who has known her and watched her grow up.

Bereavement sometimes brings a sense of the loss of a part of ourselves as well. Carol described the dynamic between herself and her husband:

> *He was always good at seeing the funny side of things and he really knew how to relax. I'm more restless, on the move all the time. I was like that before but Len would have made me sit down!*

If a relationship has been very complementary – a 'marriage of opposites' – a bereaved person may feel destabilized, unaccustomed to doing things they relied on the other person to do, or unable to *be themselves* without the other's love and influence. This dynamic may be particularly acute when a close friend dies. A teenager whose best friend died wrote to RD4U (UK bereavement charity Cruse's website for young people) with these words: 'My friend died... a massive chunk of me has been taken away...'

Sometimes we rank losses, thinking that the loss of a child or a spouse is automatically greater than the loss of any other relative or indeed a friend. One woman said, 'I haven't lost anyone close to me – only friends.' But what if the person I feel closest to – the person with whom I feel most free, most loved, most 'me' – isn't a blood relation at all but a cherished friend and soulmate? The individual feeling the greatest sense of loss at a funeral may not *necessarily* be one of those referred to (by funeral directors) as 'The Principal Mourners'; it may be the dead woman's best friend, or the dead man's unacknowledged gay partner, or the dead woman's secret lover.

Whatever the circumstances of our loss and however it affects us, adjusting to it can be bleak. Often it is only as shock wears off that the full realization of loss begins to kick in.

Matt Seaton, writing after the death of his wife, the *Observer* newspaper columnist Ruth Picardie, describes slow pain:

> *It takes not minutes, nor even months, but perhaps years for one to register and accept, at every stratum and substratum of one's being, the loss of a loved one...*
> AFTERWORD TO *BEFORE I SAY GOODBYE*

Loss can feel like the blood returning to frozen fingers as they thaw.

For some bereaved people the despair that this abject loss engenders may come a long time after the person has died. It may not start to bite until several months after the funeral – or even years later. To a bereaved person this can feel like 'going backwards'. Initially you felt you were coping, but now you feel so low you don't know what to do with yourself. Everyone told you that you were 'doing well', but now you feel more miserable than ever.

Val, who was strangely euphoric after the death of her husband Charles, found that as time went on and the euphoria subsided, she got lower and lower until she felt almost suicidal. 'About a year after he died I was utterly desolate. I felt I had nothing to live for,' she said. Val wrote several poems at this time. One of them says this:

O God, I feel I've been torn apart.
It's so hard to live alone...

Loss can be excruciatingly painful, but it may be that by acknowledging the reality of it you are actually 'coping' better than you think.

• •

These words from the book of Jeremiah (in the Old Testament) starkly express the desolation of loss:

A voice is heard in Ramah,
  lamentation and bitter weeping.

Rachel is weeping for her children;
  she refuses to be comforted for her children,
  because they are no more.
JEREMIAH 31:15

Tears and Sadness

Tears are the silent language of grief.
VOLTAIRE, *A PHILOSOPHICAL DICTIONARY*

When someone we love dies we are sad. Whatever our religious or philosophical viewpoint, however much we may believe the death was 'God's will' or 'a blessed relief', whatever cocktail of other emotions we are experiencing, we are simply and naturally sad. We wouldn't be human if this were not so.

We are sad for ourselves and what we have lost – sad for the things we can no longer do together, and no longer share. But we are also sad for the person who has died and for what they are missing. Julia, four years on from the death of her close friend Rachel, described the waves of sorrow that washed over her from time to time, particularly when she spent time with Rachel's teenage children:

> *I feel joy on her behalf at how great her kids are turning out and relief that they are well and flourishing, but I also feel terrible sadness that she isn't here to see them.*

C. S. Lewis felt a similar pain on behalf of his dead wife Joy:

> *Never, in any place or time, will she have her son on her knees, or bath him, or tell him a story, or plan for his future, or see her grandchild.*

If sadness in bereavement is universal, the way we express it will be uniquely personal. Some will internalize their sadness, dealing with it privately and silently. Others will express it in words.

Shakespeare, in the play *Macbeth*, writes:

> *Give sorrow words: the grief that does not speak*
> *Whispers the o'er-fraught heart, and bids it break.*

ACT IV, SCENE 3

Many people express sadness through tears. One woman described herself as having a seemingly bottomless well of tears after her daughter died. Some bereaved people cry openly and comfortably in the company of others, while others cry only in private. For some, tears are therapeutic – releasing, cathartic, cleansing. For others they are exhausting and debilitating.

Sheilagh cried a lot after her son Tom died. 'I mixed being active with just sitting and losing hours,' she said. 'I spent hours playing solitaire, crying, and was amazed by how wet my tears were.' She found it a great help when friends allowed her to cry in their company: 'People who risked my tears – and their own – were best of all.' By contrast, Sheilagh's husband cried less but his tears, when they came, were of an elemental, volcanic kind.

Sheilagh recalled hearing wrenching sobs coming from the kitchen where her husband had shut himself the night before Tom's funeral.

Penny recalled similar sobbing from her husband Mark after their daughter Molly died. 'He would go outside with the lawn mower and wail privately at the end of the garden,' she said.

Embarrassment, upbringing or the fear of upsetting others may make bereaved people wary of expressing their emotions publicly. Several people spoke of trying not to cry at the funeral. Sarah, bereaved in her twenties, described herself as calm and 'together' at her father's funeral until she became aware of her normally undemonstrative Uncle Stan sobbing in the pew behind her: 'It was such an alien sound. He was distraught. It made me feel very wobbly indeed.'

Carol found she couldn't cry at first when her husband Len died and that she didn't want to cry at his funeral. 'I wanted to be strong – it was something I had to get through – and I was making a speech,' she said. But later, and privately, she cried a lot. 'I find it makes me feel better – it's no good bottling it,' she said. Now, like many people in the months and years after bereavement, she finds that little things trigger tears and she 'wells up' frequently, as though her reservoir of tears is so full it easily spills over.

Louise cried a lot when her husband Andrew died, so much so that a year after his death she described herself as 'cried out'. She believed it was important for her two young children, Sam and Isabel, to see her grieve so that they understood that grief is normal, but she also tried to 'keep the lid' on her sadness when she was with them so as not to distress or frighten them.

Ros, whose husband Greg died when their two daughters were aged three and six, felt a similar need to manage her emotions when around her children but expressed her sorrow in intense wailing at night when they were asleep. Managing grief and keeping it compartmentalized may be desirable but it isn't always humanly possible. One of Ros's daughters, Hannah (now seventeen), remembers a time when, driving the route her dad used to take to work, her mum became overwhelmed with emotion and had to stop the car because she was crying too much to drive.

Not everyone cries, though. Miriam found tears an inadequate response to the loss of her husband of sixty years, quoting Wordsworth, who writes of 'thoughts which do often lie too deep for tears'. For her, tears were counterproductive and unsettling.

Some people just don't cry. They may choose not to. They may simply find they can't. Patrick said of himself after his wife's death, 'I cried, but not a lot.'

In Western culture men often find tears more difficult than women do. Some have been brought up *not* to cry. John, for example, now in his seventies, remembers being encouraged *not* to cry when his mother died when he was ten.

Blake Morrison, writing about his reactions – in adulthood – to his father's death, says this:

> *My father has always cried easily: he cried when dogs and cats died; he cried when he left my sister at her boarding-school; he cried waving goodbye from under our chestnut tree the day I went off to university. So why had he taught me to be brave and hold it in? Why have I never been able to cry? Why can't I cry for him? Even now... the tears won't come.*

Sometimes we want to weep but find we can't. Val found when her husband Charles died that at first she couldn't and didn't cry. She expressed this in a poem she wrote around this time:

> *My heart is sad*
> *But I cannot weep...*

When Val accidentally came across a cassette tape – a compilation of Charles's favourite 'singles' – and listened to it, she found herself weeping and felt a great sense of relief.

As with every other aspect of grief there is no 'right way' to do it. We need to give ourselves and others the permission to cry or not to cry, but most of all we need to allow ourselves the space to be sad.

• •

Jesus visited the grave of his dear friend Lazarus and openly expressed emotion. The book of John, chapter 11 verse 35, simply states, 'Jesus wept.'

In the Old Testament, the writer of the Psalms knew about weeping:

I am weary with my moaning;
every night I flood my bed with tears...
PSALM 6:6

Energy and Sleep

And no one ever told me about the laziness of grief. Except at my job – where the machine seems to run on much as usual – I loathe the slightest effort. Not only writing but even reading a letter is too much. Even shaving. What does it matter now whether my cheek is rough or smooth?

C. S. LEWIS

When someone dies, our normal energy levels and patterns of sleep can be severely disrupted. Some people find themselves, in the first weeks (or even months) of bereavement, feeling *more* energetic and focused than usual. Several people talked about an energy surge that got them through the first days and enabled them to handle the necessary form-filling and preparations. For some this wakefulness continues. Nick found that in the first year after the death of his wife Esther he needed very little sleep and sought the numbing effects of busyness and projects – often working late into the night. Virginia Ironside describes her friend:

> *Only a day after the death of his wife my widower friend, in a manic phase that is... common in bereaved people, suddenly lurched into wild, energetic action, wondering if he should get a job as a voluntary worker, whether he should move, whether he should get a dog...*

It is common to have difficulty sleeping after someone has died. Jackie experienced several months of sleeplessness after her son Nigel died in the Falklands War and eventually resorted to taking mild sleeping tablets. Carol, widowed in her early sixties, pushed herself physically after the death of her husband so that she would be tired enough to sleep. Hannah, whose father died when she was almost four, remembers not being able to sleep, crying at night and needing to be cuddled.

This sleeplessness can cause extreme tiredness. Grief itself can produce feelings of overwhelming exhaustion. The 'wearing off' of a period of euphoria or the sense of 'crash' that sometimes follows a burst of hyperactivity can also leave a bereaved person feeling completely wiped out. Those who have reacted by being busy and active may find themselves hitting a point of exhaustion further down the road. After the death of her husband Andrew, Louise found she 'wanted to sleep to oblivion' and that it was a monumental effort to get out of bed in the morning. For her, this exhaustion was compounded by her

'bedroom avoidance' – night after night delaying getting into an empty bed.

Jane, who in her early forties cared for both of her elderly parents when they died within months of each other and then handled the sorting out and selling of their house, described profound tiredness six months later. In common with many people, Jane found that bereavement had a knock-on effect on her own health, and that stress-related symptoms and aches and pains flared in the aftermath of her parents' death. Compromised immune systems, eczema, warts, sinus problems, itchy scalp and IBS were all mentioned by the people I spoke to, as were loss of libido or (less welcome in some cases) significantly increased libido.

With this erosion of normal physical robustness can come a sense of emotional fragility – an inability to cope with things you would normally take in your stride. The novelist Deborah Moggach writes about this, reflecting on the way she felt after her partner Mel died:

> *One feels frail and elderly, afraid of honking cars and of people shouting in the street. One dreads official letters – bank letters, parking summonses – because they seem impossibly difficult.*
> QUOTED IN *'YOU'LL GET OVER IT': THE RAGE OF BEREAVEMENT*

For some people, the feeling of having no energy can last a long time. Some writers have talked about the 'lethargy of grief' – that profound, debilitating sense of weariness and fatigue that makes even simple daily tasks absurdly hard work.

In her book *When Parents Die*, Rebecca Abrams writes, 'It is so exhausting, this feeling of lethargic misery…'

Whether or not sleep comes easily, the dreams that come with it can be a mixed bag. Some bereaved people are haunted by disturbing and destructive dreams. Novelist Blake Morrison, for example, found that after his father's death his dreams were peopled with surreal, nightmarish images:

> I dream of the vast ribcage of a bison lying on the sheet of the desert and being picked clean by vultures. I dream of blistered skin and crumbling parchment... a lost mantelpiece blowing about the sky...

Bereaved people frequently will dream of their dead loved one. They may wake in a state of distress if, in the dream, the person dies or is dead. Equally, they may wake in a state of agitation if the person has been alive in the dream and they have awoken with the expectation of seeing them again. Christine described dreams she had soon after her husband Pete died:

> I used to fall asleep on the sofa after work. It felt as if Pete was there when I was asleep and that he didn't want me to wake up again and leave him. I had to fight to wake up again.

For some, though, dreams can be a comfort, even a joy. Miriam, bereaved in her eighties after a long and happy marriage, described her dreams as bliss. Night after night in the months after Bill's death she would have happy dreams of him, so much so that she relished sleep. On the way to bed she would kiss Bill's photograph and say, 'I'm off to bed now so you come along and let's spend some time together.'

Several people talked of reassuring dreams in which the person who had died told them that all was well. Joan, who had watched her daughter Marion's slow decline with multiple sclerosis to the point at which she was bedridden for three years before her death,

was enormously comforted by a dream she had a few months after Marion died:

I was in a café and I had a strong urge to turn round. Marion was there. She was well and she said, 'Don't worry. I'm alright. I'm healed.' I was able to hug her, which I couldn't do for years because it was too painful for her.

Christine, whose husband Pete died unexpectedly during surgery, was comforted by a dream reported to her by her brother-in-law in which Pete, in a room full of machines, said, 'Tell Chris I'm alright now.'

• •

In the Old Testament, the writer of the ancient Jewish book of Psalms understands the physical impact of sorrow and expresses it powerfully:

I am utterly bowed down and prostrate;
  all day long I go around mourning.
For my loins are filled with burning,
  and there is no soundness in my flesh.
I am utterly spent and crushed;
  I groan because of the tumult of my heart.
PSALM 38:6–8

Loneliness and Yearning

The feeling of howling loneliness after a bereavement is unlike the loneliness felt at any other time.
VIRGINIA IRONSIDE

Bereavement can be a terribly lonely time. If the person who has died is your lifelong partner, or your closest companion, or your adored sister or brother, you will feel intensely lonely when death separates you from them. One woman described loneliness as an awful 'disembowelled feeling'; another, as aching longing. Linda, who had a miscarriage, talked of 'terrible emptiness'.

Those who have lost partners may dread the loneliness of an empty house, a meal for one or a holiday spent alone. They may feel that death has cut them off from a world of shared experience – from nuances, jokes and references that have no meaning for anyone else but the person who has died. They may be acutely aware of the loss of touch and intimacy. Susan Wallbank, in her book *The Empty Bed*, quotes a widow:

> *Over the past nine years I have found the loss of cuddling, kissing, hard to bear... leave alone making love. It sometimes*

seems so incredible that all my life, having enjoyed the warmth of physical contact, with first my parents, and then Bob, I am now isolated in some refrigerator of iron-grey loneliness. It is akin to solitary confinement.

Loneliness can make us yearn for reconnection. It can give us a vague, unfocused sense of searching for something. We may find ourselves roaming about, endlessly window-shopping or wandering around with a sense that something is missing. We may be overwhelmed with yearning.

 CR80

The death of someone close can be an isolating experience, and the sense of isolation may grow as time passes. A few months into bereavement people often find themselves with less company than at the time of the funeral. The initial flurry of support may have waned, and feelings of isolation and abandonment may increase. Val, bereaved after many years of marriage, found that going from being part of a couple to being a single woman with a lot of married friends was a lonely process. 'I found that as a widow I wasn't invited out as much,' she said. 'Maybe I was even perceived as a threat! And I had a sense

that people were avoiding me because they didn't know what to say.'

But even those whose friends rally round and include them in things still have to go home alone at the end of the evening. And even those who live with family and friends find bereavement a lonely process. No one else really *does* understand how you are feeling because you are unique. Because bereavement is so individual it is, essentially, solitary. Even people grieving together in families may feel lonely – especially if everyone is behaving differently.

As the months and years progress, many bereaved people develop strategies to combat their loneliness. Val identified that she felt worst on Saturdays and public holidays, when she would have done things with Charles, so she made a point of organizing outings with friends or treating herself on those days. Patrick, finding himself a fit and active widower at the age of seventy, took up new activities, such as singing in a choir, and sought other people's company by joining new clubs. 'I find that doing something – no matter what – helps with the loneliness,' he said. 'Working in the allotment and gardening is good – and I phone family and friends a lot too.' Several people mentioned gardening as a good thing to do. Others talked of the value of exercise, such as swimming, walking or yoga.

Some talked about new patterns of behaviour, about the importance of learning how to be alone and of valuing the present moment. Shelia Hancock writes very poignantly about this towards the end of her book *The Two of Us – My Life With John Thaw*:

Noticed it is a beautiful spring day. And I hate it because he can't see it. That's a waste. I have to learn to see the blossom. For myself, not just to tell John… I have always been in his shadow and never minded much when he was alive but now he's not here in person to cast the shadow and I need to get in the sun on my own.

A few months later, finding herself beginning to enjoy things again, Sheila Hancock says:

> *I'm groping my way out of the dark. I accept every invitation I get and force myself out and about. Come on, girl, get your act together. This is it. Make the most of it before you too lose it. Life, I mean.*

• •

In the Song of Songs or Song of Solomon (a book in the Old Testament that takes the form of a poetic dialogue between two lovers), one of the lovers describes the restless torment of separation:

> *Upon my bed at night*
> *I sought him whom my soul loves;*
> *I sought him, but found him not;*
> *I called him, but he gave no answer.*
> *'I will rise now and go about the city,*
> *in the streets and in the squares;*
> *I will seek him whom my soul loves.'*
> *I sought him but found him not.*
> SONG OF SONGS 3:1–2

Faith and Hope

Even though I walk through the valley of the shadow of death,
I will fear no evil, for you are with me...
PSALM 23:4

Religious faith can be a great source of strength at a time of
bereavement. Joan, reflecting on the two years since her daughter
Marion's death, said, 'How people get through this without
believing, I don't know.' Penny, whose daughter Molly died in a
road accident, said, 'Faith has held me together.' Jonathan, in his
mid-thirties and estranged from the Christian faith he'd grown up
with, found himself praying at the time of his brother Simon's
death, and increasingly values the reflective space of quiet,
contemplative worship.

All faiths acknowledge a spiritual reality underlying human
existence – an unseen dimension that makes life more than
material, human beings more than collections of atoms. At the
heart of the Christian faith is the resurrection of Jesus – a spiritual
'springtime' bursting with forgiveness and new possibilities;
goodness and life overcoming, and transforming, hatred and
despair. Christians, in common with many people of other faiths,
believe that there is more to life than what we see. They speak of
'the life of the world to come', an eternity in which broken things
will be mended; a place beyond death where there will be 'no
more crying and pain'.

For Jackie, whose son Nigel died in the Falklands War, the
Christian faith promises 'better things to come'. Although unable to
grasp or describe what heaven might be like, Jackie believes that, at
the present moment, 'We are just looking through a keyhole.'

89

Belief in resurrection and a confidence that, as the mystic writer Julian of Norwich put it, 'All manner of things will be well', helped Nick when his wife Esther died suddenly of cancer. 'Everything had been scraped away from me and I'd lost everything but everything could be rebuilt from scratch,' Nick said, remembering how he had felt about the future for himself and his four children.

Yet no matter how whole-heartedly we believe that death is a threshold to a more fulfilled, less troubled life, no matter how convinced we are that we will one day – somehow, somewhere – be reunited with the person who has died, we still feel loss and we will still need to grieve.

This tension between hope and pain, the perfect future and the flawed present, can create unique problems for Christians faced with bereavement. If I believe that my loved one is now pain-free and in the company of a loving and awesome God, is it selfish to feel sad that she is gone? If I feel lost and lonely in my bereavement, does that imply a lack of faith in eternal life? Should I mourn or celebrate?

Faith may help, but it also makes grief more complicated and may raise more questions than it answers: *Why did God let my mum die of cancer? Where are you, God, in my despair? Why did my husband suffer for so long before his death? Where is heaven? If heaven exists, does hell exist too?* Most people's belief system has holes in it. Some concepts may simply be beyond our imagination's grasp.

Sometimes, too, the experience of watching someone die causes a person of faith to question what they believe. C. S. Lewis, a well-known Christian writer, found his faith profoundly challenged by the death of his wife. 'Where is God?' he wrote in *A Grief Observed*, describing the early stages of his grief. '... go to Him when your need is desperate, when all other help is vain, and what do you find?

A door slammed in your face, and a sound of bolting and double bolting on the inside. After that, silence.'

Hope had a similar sense of being abandoned by God when her mother Edwina died traumatically. 'It feels like God has deserted you. Your prayers seem unanswered. You feel let down,' she said.

For Hannah, bereaved as a young child, her father's death from cancer has been a barrier to faith in a God of love. Now, at the age of seventeen, she does not believe such a God exists.

Even people with great faith have doubts. If faith is real and robust it must be able to contain our bewilderment. If we have a relationship with God, then honest questioning is a valid part of that relationship. The book of Psalms in the Old Testament is full of people crying out to God in raw misery.

How much longer, Lord, will you forget about me?
  Will it be forever?
How long will you hide?
How long must I be confused and miserable all day?
PSALM 13:1–2

Voicing lamentations to God is an important and often neglected part of mourning.

☙

Human beings have a deep need to make sense of the things that happen to them – to see pattern and purpose. Finding a sense of logic in a bereavement may make it easier to bear. Sarah, for example, who experienced her father's death from a brain tumour when she was in her twenties, was able to help and comfort her teenage daughter's friend Charlotte twenty years later, when Charlotte's father was suffering from a similar illness. 'I knew exactly how she felt. It gave me some sense of there being a reason for Dad's death,' she said.

Penny, whose daughter Molly died at the age of twelve, was consoled by her belief that each human being has an allotted life span and that Molly's life, however brief, was complete. 'God had only given us Molly for twelve years. Her life was a gift – it was just shorter than we'd have liked,' she said.

Some Christians maintain that everything that happens to us in life is the result of a divine will – that we are in God's hands and that, in ways we cannot yet fathom, things that seem bad are part of a bigger picture that will ultimately make sense. Other Christians believe that many things are random and that God, having made a universe that is free, suffers alongside us but rarely intervenes to alter the course of events. Wherever Christians locate themselves on this spectrum of understanding, there will always be things that are inexplicable. Louise had difficulty explaining things to her four-year-old son when his father died suddenly of a brain haemorrhage:

> *I say that Andrew is in heaven with God but I don't want Sam to hate God for taking his Daddy away. I'm happy to say to the children that I don't **know** but I believe...*

In bereavement, whatever our faith position, it is sometimes necessary to live with unanswered questions. As hospice chaplain Tom Gordon writes in *New Journeys Now Begin*:

> *Death, like life, cannot and should not be tied up with red ribbon. It does not come neatly packaged. It has to be faced with all its rough edges, unfinished business, ugliness and pain. That is what is real.*

• •

Many people believe that, even in their most desperate times, God is with them – whether or not they are conscious of it. This poem develops this idea.

> *I am with you always.*
> *When the crushing pain of doubt sets in*
> *and you feel utterly, utterly alone,*
> *I am with you.*
> *When you are screaming why at the sky*
> *and the pain sears through you*
> *like a soldier's spear,*
> *I am with you.*

When everything you had
trickles like sand through your fingers,
I am with you.
When your plans are in shreds,
I am with you.
Always
I am here.
SUE WALLACE

Support and Comfort

As a mother comforts her child,
  so I will comfort you.
ISAIAH 66:13

Although bereavement is an individual and lonely process, the actions and sensitivities of the people around us can make a huge difference to how we feel. Friends and neighbours can provide a web of support that holds us like a safety net. Their help may be practical like Sheilagh's friends, who, quietly and without fuss, dealt with the catering at her son's funeral, or like Jane's niece, who slept over on the night of Jane's mother's funeral so that she didn't have to be in an empty house. Little kindnesses, such as the 'Thinking of you' text sent to a friend on the first Mother's Day after her mum's death, or the teacher of a teenage girl warning her when hymns that had been sung at her father's funeral were coming up in school assembly, can make bereavement easier to bear. Flowers, cards and letters sent when someone dies may seem inadequate to the sender but they are often a great source of comfort to the recipient.

One woman valued the relaxation tapes a friend gave her. Another was especially grateful to the friends who invited her on holiday with them after her husband died. Some people appreciated help with childcare, or dog-walking or domestic repairs. One man welcomed his mate who turned up to drink beer and watch the football with him.

Perhaps more important than any of these acts of kindness, however, were the friends themselves. Bill found when his stepfather died that the physical, wordless presence of others was very

comforting. Most supportive of all, said Sheilagh, were 'the people who didn't shun us'.

Being with someone who is bereaved can be difficult, and many shy away from it. We may not know what to say. Our efforts to help may seem clumsy and awkward. But being there itself is what really matters, being prepared for (as Sheila Cassidy writes in *Sharing the Darkness*) 'sometimes sitting empty handed when you would rather run away'.

'People who would laugh and cry with me and share good memories really helped,' one woman said. By contrast, when her husband Pete died, Christine found that 'People who avoided talking about Pete were the most unhelpful.' Jane treasured the people who would ring up and invite her out and then, when rebuffed, would keep on asking. Nick praised the friends who were thick-skinned enough to put their own needs and egos to one side when offering support. Val appreciated the friend who just turned up unannounced because 'When you are low you can't motivate yourself to ask for help.'

Most people wanted non-judgmental support rather than advice. Many wanted not to be distracted from their grief but to be accompanied though it.

For some people, tactful, generous support isn't always easy to find. Writer Alice Jolly wrote harrowingly in *The Guardian* newspaper about people's reactions when she gave birth to a stillborn baby:

> *I didn't expect much. I didn't need flowers, or home-made shepherd's pies, or lectures about positive thinking. All I wanted was for people to look my pain in the face. So very simple – but, as I discovered, so very rare.*

• •

People who tune in to the way we are feeling can bring unimaginable comfort when we are bereaved. The apostle Paul, writing to the church in first-century Rome, encouraged empathy:

> *Rejoice with those who rejoice, weep with those who weep.*
> ROMANS 12:15

Words and Silence

At work, at the club, in the street, I see people, as they approach me, trying to make up their minds whether they'll 'say something about it' or not. I hate it if they do, and if they don't... Perhaps the bereaved ought to be isolated in special settlements like lepers.

C. S. LEWIS

'I don't know what to say...' is a common reaction when someone dies. Embarrassment, fear of saying the wrong thing, fear of triggering tears all conspire to make us evasive and euphemistic. Yet for many bereaved people the need to talk is considerable and words really do help.

'People think I don't want to talk about him,' one woman said, 'but I want to talk about him all the time!' Ros found talking to her two young daughters Hannah and Ruth after their father died very important. They talked about what had happened and about how they all felt, but most of all they talked about *him*. Patrick, bereaved a year ago, said, 'I talk at every opportunity. I like talking about Joanna.' Penny, whose daughter Molly died, said, 'Friends made me talk about Molly until I cried and I was grateful for this. It helped. A scar can't heal except from the bottom.'

Bereavement experts underline the importance of talking. 'Telling your story often and in detail is primal to the grieving process,' says Elisabeth Kübler-Ross. Putting things into words can certainly help us feel more in control, less chaotic, more 'on top of things'. Some people find that writing things down helps too. They may keep a journal or write poetry.

'It's amazing how writing down something helps,' said Joan,

who wrote a number of poems after her daughter Marion died. Val, who had never written before, began writing after the death of her husband Charles. 'Once I started I kept going. I found it very comforting,' she said. C. S. Lewis, a writer by profession, found that words helped him manage his grief when his wife Joy died. 'By writing it all down... I believe I get a little outside it,' he wrote.

Sharing our stories is a basic part of being human, and many people say they find reading about the experiences of other bereaved people compelling and therapeutic.

For some, though, words are unbearable. Carol, two years on

from the death of her husband Len, says she finds her mother-in-law's insistence on talking about Len very upsetting. This jarring of different ways of responding to death highlights the difficulties family members experience when grieving side by side. For some, talking is more helpful than for others.

There are also 'good' words and 'bad' words. Many people reported things that had been said to them that were tactless and upsetting. Linda, in the aftermath of her miscarriage, was told, 'You can always have another one' and 'It's for the best.' Louise was appalled when, less than a year after the death of her husband Andrew, someone said, 'You'll meet someone else!' Jane said, 'I hated people saying that because my parents were in their eighties when they died it was less of a blow for me.' Dave and Jackie, whose son died in the Falklands, were horrified when someone asked, 'Was he your *only* son then?' and, on being told they had two other sons, then said, 'Well that's alright then!'

Bad advice and rebukes were just as unwelcome as thoughtless – if well-intentioned – remarks. Ian, whose wife Barbara died after forty-four years of marriage, confided in Barbara's sister that on a couple of occasions after her death he had dozed off in the chair and awoken with a sense that Barbara was sitting there with him. Soon afterwards his brother-in-law rang up and angrily reprimanded Ian for what he had said, saying it had upset Barbara's sister!

For some, though, even crass or inappropriate words are better than an absence of words. Sheilagh said, 'Platitudes are better than not talking.'

Many bereaved people find the silence they encounter from others extremely difficult to cope with. Linda found it dreadful that nobody talked about her baby's death afterwards.

> 'When I came home from hospital my parents-in-law didn't say a word. It was really upsetting. They totally ignored what had happened. Now, if it happened to someone I knew I would want to give them the chance to talk – to **shout!**'

Similarly, Alice Jolly, writing in *The Guardian* newspaper about her stillborn daughter, said:

> *Less than a month after her death, it was our son's third birthday and my husband and I organized a party for him. About thirty adults attended... accompanying their children. But with the exception of two close friends, no one mentioned Laura's death. The shock of that silence was nearly as bad as the shock of my daughter's death.*

The adults attending this party no doubt assumed that Alice wouldn't want to be 'upset' by talking about her dead child. In this case they got it wrong; but because we are all different, in the case of someone else this approach may have been *right*. For some, silence can be a balm and a retreat.

Some emotions go beyond words and can only be expressed in silent gestures. Di Stubbs from Winston's Wish, talking on the BBC radio programme *Woman's Hour*, described a boy who attended a special Camp Winston for children bereaved as a result of suicide. Having thrown lumps of clay at the 'Anger Wall', the boy took the clay and made an exquisitely delicate figure of a man with a noose around his neck. Knowing that the boy's father had hanged himself, staff asked him what he wanted to do with the figure. Did he want to keep it, destroy it, or return the clay to the bucket? Wordlessly, the little boy took the knotted rope from around the figure's neck and returned only *that* to the bucket of clay. To have begun to describe in words what that gesture symbolized would have been impossible for most people of any age. Sometimes just being with somebody as they express their grief is more important than what we say.

The friend who can be silent with us in a moment of confusion or despair, who can stay with us in an hour of grief and bereavement, who can tolerate not knowing... not healing, not curing... that is a friend indeed.
HENRI NOUWEN

• •

In the book of Genesis, at the very start of the Bible, the elderly Jacob reacts to news of his son's death in gestures that go beyond words:

Then Jacob tore his clothes, put on sackcloth, and mourned for his son many days. All his sons and daughters came to comfort him, but he refused to be comforted...
GENESIS 37:34

Belongings and Changes

The dress she chose was green. She found it in
Our clothes-filled cabin trunk. The pot-pourri,
In muslin bags, was full of where and when.
I turn that scent like a memorial key.

DOUGLAS DUNN, 'EMPTY WARDROBES'

Decisions about whether to keep or discard a person's belongings
after their death, and when and how to begin to sort out clothes,
shoes and books, are as uniquely personal as everything else about
bereavement. Some people sort things out in the first weeks and
months; others wait years before they even think about moving
things or making changes. One man I knew found that on returning
to the house the day after his wife's death a well-intentioned but
interfering neighbour had removed all his wife's things so that he
'wouldn't have to think about it'. Being a gentle and magnanimous
man, he accepted this action as the kind act it was meant to be.
Others may have found it a monstrous violation. At the other
extreme, I knew an elderly man who left his wife's gardening shoes
by the back door for twenty years after her death.

People vary greatly in their attitude to 'stuff'. Some see
belongings as nothing more than unwanted jumble after a person's
death. But, much more commonly, people find that a loved one's
things acquire new significance. Favourite hats, wedding rings,
letters, cards, holiday mementoes are kept and treasured. Sometimes
surprising things become special. For Jonathan, old cassettes made
by his brother when they were teenagers became precious objects
after his brother's death. Louise found herself hoarding scraps of
paper she discovered with her husband's handwriting on them after

he died. Things, which are still 'only things', now become our last link with the physical part of a person's life. This heightened significance often causes conflict within families. Siblings may fall out over a particular keepsake of their parents: 'She promised that jug to *me*'; 'But *I* was with him when he bought that pipe'; 'She always read that story to *me* at bedtime...'

Immediately after my father's death I was obsessed with the need to have things of his to remind me of him, to keep him

alive in some way. I wanted to build a fortress of his books and clothes and pictures, and hide inside it... I was anxious lest my stepmother failed to realize how important my father's belongings were to me, anxious lest other brothers and sisters took things I felt I needed.

REBECCA ABRAMS

Some bereaved people deal quickly and unsentimentally with clothes and shoes. Val asked a friend to help her sort things a few weeks after her husband's death and gave the lot to a charity for the homeless. Nick waited several months and then – again with a friend's help – sorted his wife Esther's clothes into the garments he was especially attached to and wanted to keep, and the garments he felt unemotional about and could easily give away. At a later stage he then culled the 'kept' items again. Sue, whose husband often

worked away from home, deliberately removed his things from their wardrobe when he died so that she couldn't kid herself that he was just away on a business trip. Kathy rearranged her son's bedroom immediately after his death so that she wouldn't be tempted to make it into a shrine.

But many people don't throw anything away for a long time. Patrick, whose wife died nearly two years ago, still has all her clothing. 'I'm quite happy about that,' he says. 'She loved strong colours. When I peep in the wardrobe I get a sense of her.'

Sometimes clothes themselves can be therapeutic. Penny sorted her daughter Molly's things out very slowly with Molly's older sister. 'When we reached the point where we couldn't do it, we'd stop,' she said. 'It was actually quite a treat to touch and remember her clothes.'

Clothes can become comfort objects. Nick remembers finding his son clutching a bag of Esther's and sobbing, soon after her death. One man described how, for months after his wife died, he kept her nightdress on the pillow where he could rest his head on it and smell her scent. Smells are often very important. One woman said she couldn't bear to change her son's sheets after his death because she didn't want to wash the smell of him away. Ros, on the other hand, found that smelling her husband's clothes left her in turmoil, and if she smelled the aftershave he always wore on someone else, she would have to walk away.

Some people worry that an attachment to a particular photograph, hat or scarf is somehow unhealthy. Friends and neighbours of bereaved people may sometimes persuade them to throw things out or put them away, fearing that daily contact with a dead person's things is somehow 'prolonging their grief'. But there are no rules, and everyone is different. Queen Victoria allegedly had Prince Albert's dressing gown laid out for him on his bed every night for years after his death. If a widow leaves her husband's bathrobe on the back of the bedroom door for ten years because it comforts her, that is fine. If, on the other hand, she repaints her bedroom, gets new bed linen and moves the furniture around as an outward acknowledgment of the new reality of widowhood, that is fine too.

⋐⋑

There are already enough changes to deal with after a person's death irrespective of whether belongings are sorted quickly and methodically or gradually and haphazardly. There may be financial changes in a household, changes in domestic arrangements or changes in roles. Mike recalls his mother's hair turning white overnight when his father died when he was six and feeling suddenly different from his friends for 'not having a dad'. If a parent of young children dies, the eldest child may become a carer and surrogate parent to his or her siblings. If the practical partner in a marriage dies, a wife or husband may be left not knowing how to programme the video recorder or how to operate the lawn mower. After his wife's death, Patrick felt the need to fill the roles played by her as well as those he had always played. 'Now I need to be a father and a *mother*, a grandfather and a grand*mother*,' he said. 'Joanna was so good at things like birthday cards and I want to do things as she did them.'

In the midst of all this change and readjustment, the 'right time' to sort out the cupboards and drawers will be different for each bereaved person. Everyone has their own way of coping, and the non-bereaved are usually most helpful when they take their cue from the bereaved and resist making 'helpful suggestions'.

110

• •

Some people find rituals helpful when dealing with change and loss. You could use this 'liturgy' when sorting out belongings, adapting it to suit your situation:

These are her things,
the fabric of her life,
clothes she has worn, things she has made,
gifts she has treasured, shoes she has walked in.

These are the things I keep to remind me of her.
I am grateful for their colours and textures and smells.
I will treasure them and keep them safe.

These are the things I choose to let go of.
Some will be gifts to others, some will be recycled and used by strangers,
some will have no further use.
I am grateful for all they meant to her and for the memories that they stir
*   in me.*

I weep for what I have lost.
I cherish all I have known.
I embrace all that is still to come.

Anniversaries and Remembrances

The life of the dead is placed in the memory of the living.
CICERO, *PHILIPPICOE*

Many people say that the first year after someone's death is the worst – the first birthday, the first Christmas, the first wedding anniversary, the anniversary of the person's death. Sarah found this to be the case after her father died. 'When we'd passed the first anniversary I had a sense of moving on and started to feel better. We were no longer saying "This time last year...",' she said.

Some bereaved people find that the second or third year is worse than the first because the anaesthetizing effect of shock has worn off and the level of support and sympathy has dwindled.

Dealing with 'landmark days' in the first years can be hard. Nick had expected the first Christmas and Mother's Day to be difficult but hadn't anticipated how bad his dead wife's birthday would be for himself and their children. 'We were on holiday. I felt winded – like walking into a door I hadn't seen,' he said. Now, four years later, he anticipates this day and he and his children have a meal to celebrate Esther's birthday.

Louise had expected the first Christmas after her husband Andrew died to be difficult. 'I'd geared myself up for Christmas thinking I must get through this, but then New Year hit me like a sledgehammer,' she said.

Joan, whose daughter Marion died two years ago, also finds New Year difficult because 'It feels as if we're leaving Marion further and further behind.'

CR/RO

Marking anniversaries can be an opportunity to remember in a particular way the person who has died. Many churches hold annual 'memorial services', during which candles are lit and the names of people who have died are read aloud. Hospices often hold similar candle-lighting ceremonies for the families of people who have recently died. Conscious acts of remembrance can be useful. Ros and her children lit a candle at home on special occasions to remember her husband Greg for several years after his death. Joan lights a candle in her living room each night as a way of remembering her daughter Marion.

Children, especially very young children, often fear that they will forget the person who has died. Making 'memory boxes' containing special objects, or 'memory

jars' (in which layers of different coloured sand represent particular things the child wishes to remember) can help with this. Hannah remembers her special 'Dad' Christmas bauble that she made at a bereavement support event and that went on the Christmas tree for years after his death. Because Hannah was only three when her

father died, her mother felt that keeping his memory alive was particularly important, so photographs, keepsakes and family stories have been a big part of their life together. Nick, whose four children were also quite young when their mother died, emphasizes the importance of repeating happy stories and of helping the children have an ongoing sense of who their mother was. He writes each of them a letter on the anniversary of Esther's death, telling them things about Esther and imagining how she would react to their achievements and development.

Retrieving and holding on to good memories of a person's life is especially important when that person has died after a long illness, and it is hard to remember how they were before they were ill. If their death has been traumatic there may be difficult and painful memories to work through. One man described his young daughter, whose last contact with an angry morphine-doped mother – bearing little resemblance to her real self – had been hurtful. 'It's been necessary,' he said, 'to offset that harrowing last encounter with memories of good times.'

People remember in numerous ways: photos; a rosebush planted in the garden; a wedding ring worn on a chain around the neck; a favourite hat mounted on the wall; a folder of special things; flowers on special occasions.

Remembering is usually bittersweet. Often it is terribly painful, as these lines from a poem by Edna St Vincent Millay highlight:

There are a hundred places where I fear
To go, – so with his memory they brim!
And entering with relief some quiet place
Where never fell his foot or shone his face

I say, 'There is no memory
    of him here!'
And stand so stricken, so
    remembering him.
'TIME DOES NOT BRING RELIEF'

Holding good and painful
memories in balance can be
difficult when often one
threatens to outweigh the other.
Keeping authentic memories is
also a challenge. Sometimes our
memory of dead people
becomes distorted so that we
turn them into saints. C. S.
Lewis noticed this tendency in
himself in *A Grief Observed* ('H'
is the initial by which he refers
to his wife):

> *Already, less than a month*
> *after her death, I can feel*
> *the slow, insidious beginning*
> *of a process that will make*
> *the H. I think of into a*
> *more and more imaginary*
> *woman.*

Rebecca Abrams, bereaved as a
teenager, found this rose-tinting
especially unpalatable:

More than anything I loathed the sanctification of my father, a process that began to take place almost immediately he was dead. I knew him as bad-tempered, difficult, anti-social, allergic to physical exercise. And I knew him also as clever and sensitive and rather fun and mischievous. All of these things made up the father I loved. It was terrible to hear him turned into some kind of saint.

Some bereavement workers use an exercise to help children remember someone who has died that involves holding three stones – one ordinary, one rough and one precious. The stones represent good, bad and ordinary memories and the fact that all three can be simultaneously held, cherished and mourned.

• •

Jesus knew the power of memory. The night before his crucifixion he gave his friends a very tactile way of remembering him involving bread – a basic everyday commodity. His words probably seemed strange to his friends. Christians keep this remembrance in the service of Holy Communion.

Jesus took some bread in his hands and gave thanks for it. He broke the bread and handed it to his apostles. Then he said, 'This is my body, which is given for you. Eat this as a way of remembering me!'
LUKE 22:19

Endings and Beginnings

For my sake – turn again to life, and smile...
MARY LEE HALL, 'TURN AGAIN TO LIFE'

How long does bereavement last? When does a bereaved person stop being a bereaved person? When is it OK to laugh again? When is it appropriate to remarry?

A hundred years ago there were rules – albeit complicated ones – about the duration of 'mourning'. A woman wore black clothing for two years after the death of her husband. The parents of dead children or the children of dead parents wore black for a year; bereaved siblings for six months. Today, most employers will grant less than a week's 'compassionate leave' after a bereavement. Friends and work colleagues often expect us to be 'over it' or 'coping' within months. So what are the rules? What are 'normal' time frames?

In most cases bereavement doesn't follow any logical or sequential pattern. Its shape – if indeed it has one – is usually untidy. It isn't linear or neat. One woman said, 'There was no sense of progression. It was just jumbled up. You feel as if you've moved on and then, wham, you're back to square one.'

C. S. Lewis echoes this idea:

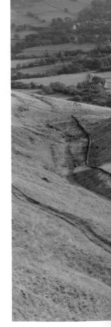

Grief is like a long valley, a winding valley where any bend may reveal a totally new landscape... Sometimes... you are presented with exactly the

same sort of country you thought you had left behind miles ago. That is when you wonder whether the valley isn't a circular trench.

Despite this, many people speak of a gradual easing of their grief – a dimming or calming of emotions, a lightening of mood. One man described himself as 'slowly resurfacing'.

How long this takes will vary for each person. Six months? Six years? Joe Lawley, one of the founders of the bereaved parents support group The Compassionate Friends, described the way

bereaved parents compared themselves with one another when meeting each other for the first time:

They'd look at you... and think, 'They're not as bad as me' and we'd look at them and think, 'We're not as bad as them.' Because the grief is difficult for you to gauge, you wonder, 'Am I getting better?'

Kay, whose grandmother died ten years ago, says, 'I still miss her now.' Carol, whose husband Len died three years ago, says, 'Maybe I'll feel better in ten years' time. Now the sense of loss is as great as ever.' Penny, whose daughter Molly died ten years ago, is very sensitive to smells that remind her of the time of year when Molly died. 'She died in March and I always feel low at the oncoming of spring.' Linda, who had a miscarriage eighteen years ago, says, 'Part of the grieving will always continue.'

By contrast, Kate Hull Rodgers had a stillborn child and, pregnant again three months later, felt she recovered quickly. She resented people's expectations that grief should last longer than it did.

People tend to project things onto you – like 'Oh, you must be feeling awful, you'll never get over it.' And your inner brain is going, 'No, actually I'm OK.' I wasn't going to let anyone tell me I should be grieving more.

QUOTED IN *RELATIVE GRIEF*

However long the process takes, most people talk less of recovery than of readjustment. They talk not of 'getting over it' so much as learning to live with it, incorporating bereavement into who they are, reinvesting in life. One woman talked of a wound becoming a scar. Sports writer Matthew Engel, whose teenage son died from cancer, said this:

We don't want to get over it. The challenge is to ensure that we can accept Laurie's death into the narrative of our lives without destroying everything else we touch.
QUOTED IN *HOW TO HAVE A GOOD DEATH*

In most cases the grieving *doesn't* stop – especially for those who have lost children or life partners. Even those who remarry continue to grieve husbands and wives within their new marriages. Hamlet criticizes his mother for the unseemly haste with which she marries his uncle Claudius. Julie faced criticism from family and friends when she met Geoff just months after her husband's death. 'His wife had died six weeks after Neil had died and he had three small children. I was unhappy on my own,' she said. 'We were both vulnerable and needy. We grieved together.' Remarriage can be an affirmation of the quality of the first marriage. Ian, widowed in his sixties, married again eighteen months after his wife's death. 'Remarrying was a major factor in helping me to recover,' he said. 'I'm as happy now as I've ever been. I'm lucky to have married two smashers!'

Sometimes bereaved people fear that if they stop grieving they will lose their loved one forever. Grief can be the last vestige of connection. Ed Farrelly said this after his wife's death:

I hope – I very much hope – that I will still in twenty or fifty years, however long I live... still get sudden uncontrollable bursts of grief, because that is a genuine reflection of my love for Nadia.
QUOTED IN *RELATIVE GRIEF*

Beginning to live once more, rediscovering an appetite for life, falling in love again or simply feeling brighter and lighter doesn't mean forgetting. It doesn't mean you love less. It is simply part of

healing. Some people might need help with this healing process, especially if they feel stuck in destructive patterns of behaviour or thoughts. There is a list of organizations and websites on pages 124–27, as well as some ideas of books that might be useful. This advice from Jeremy Howe, whose wife Elizabeth was murdered at the age of thirty-four, seems a good note to finish on.

Trust your instincts... Take each moment as it comes... And just put one foot forward at a time... you do get through it. And the advice I'd give to people – and it's terribly pat – is, it will get better. It doesn't mean you love that person any the less. It's just that time passes and you adjust to it.

QUOTED IN *RELATIVE GRIEF*

122

• •

Tom Gordon, chaplain at an Edinburgh hospice, has written his own version of the Bible passage quoted on page 38, Ecclesiastes 3:1–8.

The Seasons of Grief

Every stage of grief has its season,
And every facet of loss has its time.

A time for disbelief, and a time for harsh reality.
A time to know, and a time to be consumed by unknowing.
A time for clarity, and a time of uncertainty.
A time for public smiles, and a time for private tears.
A time to be thankful, and a time of regret.
A time of giving up, and a time for going on.
A time of living half a life, and a time of wanting to live again.
A time of then, and a time of now.
A time to feel hopeless, and a time to be positive.
A time of looking forward, and a time of wanting life to end.
A time of faith, and a time of doubt.
A time for holding on, and a time for letting go.
A time when steps are light, and a time when limbs are tired.
A time of hazy memories, and a time of instant recall.
A time for living with death, and a time for living with life.
A time of fruitfulness, and a time of growth.
A time of despair, and a time of purpose.
A time of emptiness, and a time of hope.
A time for rage, and a time for peace.

Books You May Find Helpful

Rebecca Abrams, *When Parents Die*, Harper Collins, 1995.

Neil Astley (ed.), *Do Not Go Gentle: Poems for Funerals*, Bloodaxe Books, 2003.

Emily Brontë, *Wuthering Heights*, Penguin Classics, 2004.

Elizabeth Collick, *Through Grief*, DLT/Cruse, 1986.

Douglas Dunn, *Elegies*, Faber and Faber, 1985.

Jane Feinmann, *How to Have a Good Death*, Dorling Kindersley, 2006.

Tom Gordon, *New Journeys Now Begin*, Wild Goose, 2006.

Sheila Hancock, *The Two of Us: My Life with John Thaw*, Bloomsbury, 2004.

Virginia Ironside, *'You'll Get Over It': The Rage of Bereavement*, Penguin Books, 1997.

Clare Jenkins and Judy Merry, *Relative Grief*, Jessica Kingsley, 2005.

Elisabeth Kübler-Ross, *On Death and Dying*, Collier Paperbacks (USA), 1970.

Elisabeth Kübler-Ross and David Kessler, *On Grief and Grieving*, Simon and Schuster, 2005.

Tony Lake, *Living with Grief*, Sheldon Press, 1984.

C. S. Lewis, *A Grief Observed*, Faber and Faber, 1961.

Blake Morrison, *And When Did You Last See Your Father*, Granta, 1993.

Colin Murray Parkes, *Bereavement*, Pelican Books, 1975.

Colin Parry, *Tim: An Ordinary Boy*, Hodder and Stoughton, 1994.

Justine Picardie, *If the Spirit Moves You*, Picador, 2001.

Ruth Picardie, *Before I Say Goodbye*, Penguin Books, 1998.

Lily Pincus, *Death and the Family*, Faber and Faber, 1976.

Joyce Rupp, *Praying Our Goodbyes*, Ave Maria Press, 1988.

Antoine de Saint-Exupéry, *Flight to Arras*, Macmillan, 1975.

Nicola Slee, *Easter Garden*, Fount Paperbacks, 1990.

Susan Wallbank, *The Empty Bed*, DLT, 1992.

Laurence Whistler, *The Initials in the Heart*, Hart-Davis, 1964.

Wise Traveller: Loss, Scripture Union, 2007.

Books Written for Children

Debi Gliori, *No Matter What*, Bloomsbury, 2003.

Laurene Krasny Brown and Marc Brown, *When Dinosaurs Die: A Guide to Understanding Death*, Little Brown and Company, 2004.

Michaelene Mundy, *Sad Isn't Bad: A Good Grief Guidebook for Kids Dealing with Loss*, University of Massachusetts Press, 2004.

Michael Rosen and Quentin Blake, *Michael Rosen's Sad Book*, Walker Books, 2004.

Doris Stickney, *Waterbugs and Dragonflies*, Geoffrey Chapman, 2004.

Susan Varley, *Badger's Parting Gift*, Picture Lions, 1994.

Winston's Wish, *Muddles, Puddles and Sunshine*, Hawthorn Press, 2007.

List of Organizations and Websites

The Compassionate Friends
53 North Street
Bristol BS3 1EN
Helpline: 0117 953 0630
www.tcf.org.uk

Cruse Bereavement Care
126 Sheen Road
Richmond
Surrey TW9 1UR
Tel: 020 8940 4818
www.crusebereavementcare.org.uk

RD4U (Cruse Bereavement Care's Website for Young People)
www.rd4u.org.uk

FACTS Health Centre (Offer counselling, advice and support if someone
has died after being ill from AIDS)
126 Sheen Road
Richmond
Surrey TW9 1UR
Tel: 020 8348 9195

The Foundation for the Study of Infant Deaths (Cot Death Research and
Support)
14 Halkin Street
London SW1X 7DP
Tel: 020 7233 8001
Cot Death Helpline: 020 7233 2090 (24 hours)

The Miscarriage Association
c/o Clayton Hospital
Northgate
Wakefield
West Yorkshire WF1 3JS
Tel: 01924 200 799
www.miscarriageassociation.org.uk

The National Association of Widows
48 Queens Road
Coventry CV1 3ER
Tel: 024 7663 4848
www.nawidows.org.uk

Road Peace (The United Kingdom's national charity for road crash victims provides support to those bereaved or injured in a road crash)
PO Box 2579
London NW10 3PW
Tel: 020 8838 5102
Support line: 020 8964 1021
www.roadpeace.org

The Samaritans
Tel: 08457 90 90 90 for the cost of a local call.
In the Republic of Ireland – 1850 60 90 90 for the cost of a local call
www.samaritans.org.uk

The Stillbirth and Neonatal Death Society (SANDS),
28 Portland Place
London W1N 4DE
Helpline: 020 7436 5881
www.uk-sands.org

The War Widows Association of Great Britain
c/o 48 Pall Mall
London SW1Y 5JY
Tel: 0870 2411 305
www.warwidowsassociation.org.uk

Winston's Wish – The Charity for Bereaved Children
The Clara Burgess Centre
Westmoreland House
80–86 Bath Road
Cheltenham
Gloucestershire GL53 7JT
Helpline: 08452 03 04 05
General Enquiries: 01242 515157
www.winstonswish.org.uk

Picture Acknowledgments

p. 3 Donata Pizzi/Getty Images Ltd; p. 4–5 Brand X Pictures;
p. 7 Ulf Sjostedt/Getty Images Ltd; p. 10 Lion Hudson;
p. 13 SIGRID DAUTH Stock Photography/Alamy; p. 17 Andy Rous;
p. 18 Digital Vision; p. 23 Nicholas Rous; pp. 26–27 mediacolor's/Alamy;
p. 30 Jeremy Liebman/Getty Images Ltd; p. 32 Jon Sparks/Alamy;
p. 35 Digital Vision; p. 36 Digital Vision; pp. 38–39 Herbert Kehrer/zefa/Corbis;
pp. 42–43 Thomas Dobner/Alamy; pp. 44–45 Andy Rous;
p. 49 Kuttig - People/Alamy; pp. 50-51 Andy Rous; p. 52 John Kelly/Alamy;
p. 57 Gari Wyn Williams/Alamy; p. 58 Digital Vision;
pp. 62–63 George Disario/CORBIS; pp. 64–65 Ashley Cooper/Corbis;
p. 67 Digital Vision; p. 70 Digital Vision; p. 73 Mike Goldwater/Alamy;
p. 74 Rainman/zefa/Corbis; p. 76 Digital Vision; p. 79 Andy Rous;
p. 82 Philip Brittan/Alamy; pp. 84–85 LaCoppola-Meier/Getty Images Ltd;
p. 86 Christian Kober/Alamy; p. 91 DAJ/Alamy; p. 92 Gavin Gough/Alamy;
p. 97 Charles Krebs/CORBIS; p. 101 Benelux/zefa/Corbis; p. 102 Digital Vision;
p. 107 Andy Rous; p. 108 Andy Rous; p. 113 Getty Images Ltd;
pp. 114–15 Carol Marples; pp. 116–17 Andy Rous;
pp. 118-19 eye35.com/Alamy; p. 122 Nicholas Rous.